FIGHT! FIGHT!

DISCOVERING YOUR INNER STRENGTH
WHEN BLINDSIDED BY LIFE

My Personal Battle and Fight with Cancer

D1316603

BY SYLVIA HATCHELL

FOREWORDS BY ROY WILLIAMS
AND ANNE GRAHAM LOTZ

To inquire for information about speaking engagements, please contact the UNC Women's Basketball Office at 919-962-5187 or send an email to jhigh@unc.edu.

To make a contribution to the Lineberger Comprehensive Cancer Center/ UNC Cancer Care please send donations to:

UNC Lineberger
CB 7295
Chapel Hill, NC 27599

www.unclineberger.org/giving
919-966-5905

In loving memory of my parents.

My parents, Carroll Costner Rhyne and Veda Elvira Shepard Rhyne, were the best parents anyone in this world could ever be blessed to have—wonderful, loving, caring, giving Christian parents who always saw the best in everyone and in every situation. They taught me to love God, work hard, be honest and treat others the way you wanted to be treated. The greatest blessing of my life was to be born to Carroll and Veda Rhyne.

In tribute to two great mentor coaches, Kay Yow and Dean Smith.

They loved the game of basketball, but they loved their players and the people they were associated with through basketball even more. They always gave unselfishly to players, coaches, officials and everyone they knew. The game is the great game it is today because of the example of these two great people and coaches.

- PRAISE FOR *FIGHT! FIGHT!* -

"I met Sylvia Hatchell in 1994 when I was working at ESPN and her Tar Heels won the NCAA National Championship. When I interviewed her I could tell that she was a women who had an incredible perspective on life. We've been good friends ever since. I called her often during her fight with leukemia and always hung up the phone feeling the same way I had when we first met more than a decade before. Inspired. Thank you and bless you, Sylvia, for transparently sharing your story and empowering others to overcome whatever challenges they may be facing."

-Robin Roberts, Good Morning America

"I have known Coach Hatchell for a long time. Each time I talk to Coach, her joy and positivity is inspiring. I leave each conversation with her encouraged. I know that her story—and this book—will inspire thousands of people the same way that she constantly inspires me. This book is a must-read for anyone who is facing an obstacle and needs a guide to help them discover their inner strength. Coach Hatchell is one of those special individuals whom I have turned to for advice, motivation, or inspiration in the very best of times and worst of times. In her journey and in this book, Coach Hatchell passes that caring along to every reader."

-Bev Perdue, 73rd governor of North Carolina, first female governor of the state

"I have known and admired Coach Hatchell's dedication to patients and families dealing with cancer for years. She has been a wonderful supporter of UNC Lineberger Comprehensive Cancer Center with a particular emphasis on kids with cancer. But my respect, admiration and affection for her rose again watching the remarkable way she has dealt with her own cancer journey. From the initial shock to the joy of her being cancer-free, she has been an inspiration to all. We knew she was a fighter and instilled that will to win in her team. But her dedication to the power of positive thinking was remarkable through some tough times. Her determination to keep her head held high and her body moving surely contributed to her timely recovery. Her story will be an inspiration to all who read this new book."

-Shelley Earp, director of UNC Cancer Care

"Coach Hatchell has always moved me with her courage, humility, humor, and determination. She's mentored hundreds of young women to achieve their dreams and now, by sharing her deeply personal journey of fear, pain, passion, and perseverance, she's inspiring countless men and women off the court in the fight of their lives. This story of her battle with cancer is a lesson in love and friendship, as well as how she overcame the loss of control to beat this deadly disease. I am awed to witness her strength, and overjoyed to see Coach winning her most heroic battle."

-Debra Morgan, WRAL-TV anchor and reporter

"I have had the privilege of knowing and working with numerous outstanding and successful coaches. None are more inspiring than Sylvia Hatchell. Her positive attitude and magnificent spirit will challenge you to find your best inner self amid any of life's storms. Sylvia is special, and so is her story."

-John Swofford, commissioner of the Atlantic Coast Conference

"I've always known Coach Hatchell to be a fighter, long before her battle with leukemia. She fought so many battles throughout her coaching career in order for her players to have the best opportunities in life. I remember going to visit her at UNC's Lineberger Cancer Center, and she was sitting on a chair in her room, dressed in gym clothes. I know for a fact that she fought the doctors so she wouldn't have to wear a hospital gown. We went for a walk that day through the hospital, which was her normal daily exercise routine. She literally outpaced me! Simply put, she's a fighter, and no one and nothing will ever be able to put her fire out! I will always love, respect, and admire the fight in—as I fondly call her—'Mama Hatchell.'"

-Charlotte Smith, women's basketball head coach at Elon University, NCAA champion (1994 Tar Heels)

"When I think of all of the players and coaches that I admire, Coach Sylvia Hatchell always rises to the top. She is a gem of a person: honest, trustworthy, positive and a true leader of our sport. When I spend time with her, I am encouraged and empowered to not only be a great leader, but also a great person of character. She is bright light in a sometimes dark world, and I am grateful to know her and her inspiring story."

-Dana Hart, president and CEO of the Women's Basketball Hall of Fame

"Coach Hatchell is one of the most incredible, original, loving people I have ever met. Her positive attitude, her experience and knowledge, her principals and faith, and most importantly, her love and constant desire to help others, are truly contagious. For those of us who have had the privilege to know Coach on a personal level, this book provides a true testament of a person who has been blessed with resilience, a strong will, and determination to win in life while coaching and inspiring others to do the same."

-Claudio Battaglini, director of the Integrative Exercise Oncology Laboratory and the Get REAL & HEEL Breast Cancer Rehabilitation Program

"Sylvia Hatchell knows how to win and how to inspire other people to be winners also, whether on the court or playing field, in an arena, or in a chemo chair. I've known her for almost two decades, and I have watched her bring rare and exceptional determination to each battle. That rare and exceptional determination is one of the reasons she is the winningest active women basketball coach on the planet! Her inspirational book is strategy-focused and full of tips and tactics. She's got a Southern upbringing so, of course, the book is written to 'bless your heart!'"

-Cecilia Budd Grimes, author of the **What It Means to Be Southern** *book series*

"Coach Hatchell is a survivor of acute myeloid leukemia, one of the worst types of cancer there is. When she was getting intense chemotherapy for her disease, I was awestruck by her fight and determination and how she refused to give in to side effects or negative thinking. She has been an inspiration to so many of our patients with cancer, and her book shows her strength and optimism."

-Ned Sharpless, director of UNC Lineberger Comprehensive Cancer Center

"Sylvia Hatchell: my favorite all time 'yo-yo.' Every time she has been knocked down, she comes right back up because of her strong faith. That's why I call her my 'Minister of Faith,' and you will understand that statement when you read her book."

-Albert Long, speaker, author, only four-sport letterman in ACC history

"I have been blessed to call Sylvia Hatchell my friend for many years. I have seen her mental and physical determination firsthand while learning the game of golf and while coaching basketball. More importantly, her unwavering faith in God has given her the inner strength to overcome the obstacles of illness and other challenges in her life. Sylvia's journey is a must-read; her positive attitude and courage will truly inspire you as it has me."

-Peggy Kirk Bell, LPGA pioneer, voted one of the five most influential women in golf, owner of Pine Needles and Mid Pine Resort, Pinehurst, North Carolina

"Coach Hatchell has been a dear friend of mine for many years. It was her exuberance with life, positive outlook on every situation, and deep inner strength, which comes from her unwavering faith in God, that first attracted me, and that continues to inspire me daily. Like most of us, she has known adversity, but she uses it as a steppingstone to rise to a new level. Her philosophy in life is: 'If life gives you lemons, make lemonade.' I'm so excited that her story is being shared through this book because I know there are thousands of folks who have overwhelming obstacles in their lives and will be inspired by Coach Hatchell's story to discover their own inner strength."

-Dianne Glover, friend, retired registered nurse at UNC's Division of Vascular Surgery

"Having known Coach Hatchell for over thirty-five years and having the privilege and honor to be a caregiver during her leukemia treatment, I understand firsthand how she was successful in the biggest battle of her life. This book documents Coach Hatchell's battle with acute myeloid leukemia, but more importantly it is a book of inspiration and the importance of a positive attitude when facing insurmountable odds. Although I was there to be a caregiver, I came away from that experience with more than I ever would have imagined—which is exactly what you will take with you after reading her book, *Fight! Fight!* She is as inspiring as Coach Valvano with his "never give up" speech and Kay Yow in her stoic and inspiring battle against breast cancer and the importance of working toward a cancer cure."

-Kathy Streeter Morgan, retired basketball and volleyball coach, teacher and assistant principal at Hendersonville High School in Hendersonville, North Carolina

"I've been blessed to know Coach Hatchell many years and have experienced her fighting spirit numerous times. I owe her so much, but am especially grateful for her persistence in helping my mom (Sylvia Strickland) as she battled cancer. She and my mom were extremely close for years. The cancer took my mom's life on January 17, 1997; however, while local doctors gave her only months, Sylvia took action in getting my mom better care by connecting her with the doctors at

UNC, which allowed us to enjoy our time together over several more years. From the heartfelt eulogy Sylvia gave to a crowded church at my mom's funeral, to other memories that are too many to count, I will be forever thankful for her dedication, friendship, and fighting spirit that I've loved for years!"

-Mary Lou Garnett, daughter of Coach Hatchell's administrative assistant, Sylvia Strickland, at Francis Marion University

"I have had the privilege of knowing Coach Hatchell since her diagnosis. She fought her leukemia with the same tenacity and 'never quit' spirit that she shows on the court. Her fight was an inspiration to many who never saw her give up. This book will be a continuation of that fight and spirit. I am honored to continue to call Coach Hatchell a friend. She has a caring and giving spirit that reflects in everything she does."

-Jen Kelly, former nurse practician to Dr. Pete Voorhees

"Throughout the thirty years that I have known Coach Hatchell, I have always been amazed at her fierce competitiveness and highly positive attitude, both in coaching her team and her personal life. When she was diagnosed with leukemia, I had no doubt that this competitiveness and positive attitude would enable her to fight through and beat the disease...and it did! Each time I speak with her, she continues to inspire me, and her story in this book will be an inspiration to everyone who reads it."

-Dr. Beth Miller, retired University of North Carolina senior woman administrator and as senior associate director of athletics

"Sylvia has always been a winner in the game of life. Her enthusiasm, confidence, determination, and competitive spirit are trademarks that have allowed her to excel. From our early childhood, I knew she would accomplish much. Her tenacity for life and her perseverance even in the face of adversity are attributes I greatly admire. Perhaps nothing has ever shaken her to the core more than her leukemia diagnosis. Yet, her faith never wavered. She faced her 'demon' courageously and vowed to be victorious—defeat for her was not an option. She continues to inspire others with her 'I can and I will' attitude. Through this book, she will be instrumental in encouraging others to face similar trials with persistence and hope."

-Patsy Davis, childhood friend of Sylvia Hatchell from Gastonia, North Carolina, retired director of gifted services at Gastonia County School Systems

"No one escapes life! My dear friend, Sylvia Hatchell, is no exception. Her willingness to share this journey through the darkest of days speaks to her inner strength—her faith and willingness to help others. Whether one's challenges are illness, death, emotional turmoil, or disappointments, this lovely book will inspire, enable, and give a person the 'fight' to emerge victorious. It is a must read."

-Paula Ryan, retired corporate vice president of Southeastern Regional Medical Center Corporation and currently a real estate broker in Myrtle Beach, South Carolina

"Any and all who are acquainted with Coach Sylvia Hatchell know what a driven, purpose-filled life she leads. She approaches her professional, personal, and spiritual life with gusto and a dedication to being simply the best. In this book, Coach Sylvia Hatchell takes you on a personal journey with her as she fights a devastating diagnosis of acute myeloid leukemia. From a position of powerlessness to empowerment, Sylvia Hatchell invites you to walk alongside her as she constructs the most positive and rigorous game plan possible to battle for her life and future. You cannot help but be impacted by Coach Hatchell's open and candid account of one of the darkest and most challenging times in her life."

-Jackie Koss, advanced practice nurse practitioner

"I worked directly with Coach Hatchell for six years at UNC, and I always found her to be a source of inspiration both for her team, and more broadly for the entire campus. Her enthusiasm is contagious; her love of her students and the Tar Heel community was evident through her words and actions in support of excellence. Coach Hatchell's story of battling cancer with everything she has—her faith, family, community, and team—is a story that resonates with people of all backgrounds. I admire her ability to maintain her positive attitude in the face of daunting odds. I just love her story. Keep fighting, Coach!"

-Margaret (Peggy) Jablonski, president of Jablonski Consulting Group, and former vice chancellor at University of North Carolina-Chapel Hill

"This book is another perfect example of how much Coach Hatchell cares about other people. Even after going through her own personal hardship she's sharing her experience to help encourage others. What an incredibly selfless and inspiring woman! Her strength and will power to overcome her battle with cancer is a great story and her book is a must read on how she and you can overcome any obstacle!"

-Camille Little, former UNC women's basketball player, WNBA player for the Connecticut Suns

"I have had the pleasure of knowing Coach Hatchell since I was an eighth grader growing up in Hartsville, South Carolina. As she did then, and every time since meeting her, her enthusiasm and competitiveness oozes from her. Even during this fight for her life, she remained a close friend who thought of my needs first, always encouraging me and sharing her diehard faith. Anyone who wants an insight into her positive formula for life needs to read this book."

-Beth Bass, former CEO of the Women's Basketball Coaches Association

"For over fifty years I have been privileged to observe and interact with Sylvia Hatchell on her life's journey. Strength of character inspired by a commitment to excellence has enabled her to rise to the top of her profession. A deeply-ingrained faith fueled by a positive attitude, unwavering hope, dogged determination, and superb medical treatment has allowed her to overcome a monster battle with acute myeloid leukemia; and she did it while encouraging others. She has modeled what it means to fight on the way to healing and renewed health. Hopefully many will be encouraged and challenged to develop and nurture their inner strength from her powerful story as shared in this timely book."

-Dr. Johnny E. Ross, retired minister and longtime friend of Sylvia Hatchell (retired from North Carolina Baptist State Convention)

"Coach Sylvia Hatchell is an inspiration to many people. I've heard countless stories of her positive impact over the years. She is a woman of deep faith and honorable character. She lives with an optimistic attitude, courage, and perseverance. Sylvia is an encouragement to me and surely will be to anyone who reads about her experience."

-Reverend Roger Mathis, Unity Baptist Church, Gastonia, North Carolina

"I have known Coach Sylvia Hatchell as a co-worker and as a personal friend for over forty years. Each time I talk with Sylvia, I find that her strength, enthusiasm, and positive attitude are contagious. She is a role model for all walks of life—the good times and the hard times. She knows that she does not walk alone. She wants to share her journey of faith with anyone who is facing an obstacle and needs a guide to help them discover their inner strength."

-Eleanor Rogers Burns, former coordinator of annual giving, Francis Marion University/Foundation

"*The Power of Positive Thinking, Praying, Believing,* and *Living* easily could have been the title of Coach Hatchell's book. What a story! What a life! What a legend! Sylvia Hatchell is one of my heroes. Every time I'm around her, or read her words, I'm inspired. Need encouragement? Inspiration? Here's your book!"

-J. Randall O'Brien, president of Carson-Newman University (Coach Hatchell Alma Mater)

"When I first heard about Coach Hatchell's cancer diagnosis, I had no doubt in my mind that she would beat it. I knew she would defeat it because she's a fighter. She's a strong woman, who doesn't back down from any obstacle. I believe this book will inspire many people to push through obstacles by tapping into their own inner strength, just as Coach Hatchell has done."

-LaQuanda Barksdale Quick, assistant women's basketball coach, Winston-Salem State University, and former UNC women's basketball player and WNBA player

"I have watched and admired Coach Hatchell for many years as one of the premier women's basketball coaches in NCAA Division I. She has inspired thousands of young women to be the best they can be. But my admiration for her grew exponentially as I watched her courageously, graciously, and selflessly battle through the most challenging 'game' of her life: fighting leukemia. As her caretaker and dear friend she inspired me to be a better nurse and person. This book will inspire and challenge anyone who reads it to focus on the positive and call on his or her inner strength to overcome adversity. I am blessed to have Sylvia Hatchell in my life. She truly is my hero."

-Jill Humphries, oncology nurse at UNC Cancer Care

"As Sylvia's friend and physician, I've been awed by her inner strength when faced by life's challenges which would have made others wither. Her faith in God and her insistence in putting the well-being of others ahead of herself are her defining characteristics. She never gives up—on anything. Her players see her inner strength and are tremendously inspired by it. I must admit: I am inspired by Sylvia every day."

-Dr. Harold Pillsbury, Thomas J. Dark distinguished professor of UNC otolaryngology/head and neck surgery

"Twenty-two years ago a little five-year-old boy walked into my kindergarten class and little did I know how that day would impact my life. That was the day I met Sylvia as the parent of this child, and twelve years later I was honored to become her executive assistant. Through that process I found a friend that was most genuine, most generous, caring for others more than you could imagine, and a person that always saw life in such a positive light. I encourage you to meet this person through this book that changed my life forever and will also impact yours without a doubt. I have walked with her daily for the last nine years and have not seen her waiver from that same genuine person that I met twenty-two years ago."

-Jane High, executive assistant to Coach Sylvia Hatchell

"I first met Sylvia in 1974 while in graduate school at the University of Tennessee. Our love for coaching basketball created an instant bond and a lifetime friendship evolved. I have never met a more generous, kind, nurturing, and spiritual individual. Family and friends are her lifeline. Her faith and perseverance guided her through the fight of her life, and I am so pleased that she is sharing that fight with others in this book."

-Judy Rose, director of athletics at
University of North Carolina-Charlotte

"When my wife and I heard that Coach Hatchell was diagnosed with acute myeloid leukemia, we were shocked. But then I remembered seeing all the positive sayings in her office and on Carolina women's basketball t-shirts over the years. And then we thought about her positive attitude and her faith and how she has always inspired her players. The tools she used to do that would now help her in her battle, a battle that we were confident she would win...and she did. This book will inspire many others in their life battles, and I encourage you to read and share its message with others."

-Ed "Charlie Brown" Weiss, host of "On the Beach
with Charlie Brown"

"I first met Coach Hatchell as a young high school coach at Pat Summitt's basketball camp at the University of Tennessee. Since then I have known her to have a never-ending drive to help others. Whenever she became sick with leukemia, she never wavered from that strong commitment to excellence, nor did she lose faith in her ability to overcome the illness. She always 'finds a way.' She once told me that her glass was not just half full; it was overflowing. That's how she lives, even when she is in the midst of a deadly disease, fighting for her life."

-Gina S. Markland, compliance and planned giving officer at Coastal Educational Foundation of Coastal Carolina University

"When I was playing for Coach Hatchell, two of our main slogans were 'Don't Blink' and 'Catch Us If You Can.' On the court, the meaning behind those quotes was that we were an up-tempo, transition team. If you blinked you would miss us and if you were behind us, you'd never catch us. The same, however, is true with Coach Hatchell in her life. She is constantly on the go, defying odds, supporting her players, and kicking leukemia to the curb. Leukemia blinked and couldn't catch Coach Hatchell. I use this as an example because as players, Coach always tried to relate basketball to life and through her fight with leukemia she never blinked and never let anything negative catch her. Throughout my own coaching career, Coach Hatchell has mentored me to find my inner strength."

-Meghan Austin, head women's basketball coach at Montreat College, former player for the University of North Carolina

"I am fortunate to have known Sylvia Hatchell for fifty years. From the time our friendship started back in high school, Sylvia's transparent and genuine faith in our Lord and Savior Jesus Christ has been an inspiration to me. Throughout her years of success and triumph, she has attributed His love and grace for her wonderful blessings. It comes as no surprise that Sylvia fervently counted on her Christian beliefs for strength and understanding throughout her struggle with leukemia. For anyone facing insurmountable obstacles in your life right now, Sylvia's book will inspire and create in you a tenacious spirit of joyful momentum throughout your difficult journey. Read and embrace!"

-Mary Clouse, educator for W.A. Bess Elementary School in Gastonia, North Carolina

"My friendship with Coach Hatchell goes back three generations, rooted in family ties on adjoining farms in Dallas, North Carolina.

Through those connections of living, working, and playing basketball, I know her character to be built on these four cornerstones: loyalty, faith, hard work, and determination. These traits have led her to a successful career as both a coach and mentor to countless young women. From these same characteristics, she has found the strength and resolve to win championships and to fight her most difficult battle yet, the one against leukemia. I know of no other person who could reach within to find the courage to accomplish this. Her story is an inspiration to all."

-Dottie McKinney, library assistant at Brooks, Pierce, McLendon, Humphrey & Leonard, LLP

"Knowing Sylvia for more than forty years, I have been inspired and blessed, as I have witnessed her infectious will, her fight, and her perseverance in her life. The impact she has brought to my life and to the many lives of others she has touched is infinite, whether it has been to a player, coach, colleague, boss, wife, mother, daughter, or friend. This book is a glimpse of Sylvia, the person, and her inspiring story and "fight" to be Christlike as she deals with the biggest obstacle she has ever encountered. A must read for all!"

-Judith Stroud, owner of Stroud State Farm Insurance Agency, Inc., Hendersonville, North Carolina

"Sylvia has been preparing for this battle all her life. Family, friends, and her faith have made the difference for her. And throughout her life those are the exact elements she has valued and nourished. Good for her for writing this book to tell her story and what those relationships mean to her."

-Richard Baddour, former athletic director at the University of North Carolina-Chapel Hill

"Sylvia Hatchell has been an inspiration to me as a friend and colleague for over ten years. In this book, Sylvia's steadfast faith, caring spirit, and inspirational attitude are evident as she describes her battle with cancer. Sylvia encouraged me to follow my dreams and adopt my son, Luke. Everything she does—whether it is supporting a friend, opening her home to strangers, or running a blueberry patch for Lineberger Cancer Center—is a testament to her as a selfless, caring, and loving human being. Her life story and the attitude she exhibits in every facet of her life will profoundly influence every reader of her book and will be a blessing to those struggling with their own battles."

-Kathy Marlowe, educator in health promotion at AC Reynolds High School, Asheville, NC and mountain friend

"For the past twenty years I have been blessed to call Sylvia Hatchell my dear friend. I would encourage anyone to read Sylvia's book to see how her passion for life, family, friends, and faith have helped her defeat her toughest opponent."

-Maureen A. Buck, president of Wealth Management Consultants, LLC

"Coach Hatchell is one of the most positive and influential people that we know. She always finds the silver lining in every dark cloud; there's always something positive to gain from every situation. Battling through leukemia was only another way for her to demonstrate her faith in God and to show that through God all things are possible. She is definitely one of the strongest people that we have ever met in our lives, and we are very fortunate to have the opportunity to call her our friend. I am certain that you will find her book as inspiring as she is in person!"

-Gene Pope and Nancy Pope, professional four-time USA Shag Grand National master champions (Gene is a retired fire captain and Nancy is a retired community educator)

- TABLE OF CONTENTS -

- FOREWORD -

by Roy Williams,
University of North Carolina men's basketball coach

Because of my and Sylvia's shared passion for the Lineberger Comprehensive Cancer Center, I sponsor a fundraising breakfast each year named "Fast Break Against Cancer," with the proceeds directed to Lineberger and the fight against cancer. I began the breakfast in 2004. At the 2015 breakfast, seven months after the death of legendary UNC head coach Dean Smith, Sylvia had the idea to auction off his chair. Coach Smith had used the chair for a couple of decades, which included Michael Jordan's years. Sylvia then used the chair after the men's team moved from Carmichael Arena to the Smith Center in 1986. Her idea raised $15,000.

Dr. Mark Graham, a former UNC professor who was integral in the development of the UNC breast cancer program, purchased the chair with the intent of putting it next to the chair of another legendary head coach, the late Kay Yow (whose doctor was actually Dr. Graham), so cancer patients could sit in the chairs during their chemotherapy treatments at his office. I thought this was the neatest idea.

The chairs were used for many years by Dean Smith, Kay Yow, and Sylvia Hatchell. All are Hall of Famers. But more than that, all are an inspiration—not only because of their coaching but also because of how they lived their lives.

I came to appreciate Sylvia first, for her part in bringing women's basketball to the attention of the sports world. Kay Yow, Pat Summitt, and yes, Sylvia Hatchell, were instrumental in making sure women had the same chances to participate, as men had long enjoyed. She was right there in the fight to put women's sports on an equal footing with men's. Besides that, we both love to coach fast-break basketball, and her teams are fun to watch. Her ACC championships and NCAA championship and her leadership secured her a spot in the Naismith Memorial Basketball Hall of Fame. I was pleased to be there during her induction weekend.

But I had no idea of the fight she would put up against cancer. She was diagnosed with acute myeloid leukemia shortly after I was told that I probably had cancerous tumors on both of my kidneys. Mine turned out to be benign, but I knew how awful it was to hear the doctor say the word: cancer. When I first heard about her diagnosis, I called her, thinking to encourage her. She had already decided to "fight, fight, fight," in her words. She did not dwell on it and met the challenge head on, determined to win. She exercised every day in the hospital. When people called, she turned the conversation toward raising money to find a cure. When she heard of others in the same fight, she encouraged them. She did not just talk about it; she did it every day and was a great example for other people.

With this book, she continues to do that today. Thanks, Sylvia, for your words of encouragement and for once again leading the fight.

- FOREWORD -

by Anne Graham Lotz,
Christian author and speaker

Sylvia Hatchell is not just a Hall of Fame basketball coach; she is a Hall of Faith life coach. I started reading this book and couldn't put it down until I was finished. Every word she writes is worth reading. It humbled me. Convicted me. Encouraged me. Uplifted me. Instructed me. It also opened my eyes in a fresh way to the depth of Sylvia's character.

I can't remember when I first met Sylvia Hatchell. I've known her for years simply because my husband, as a former player, was a member of the elite UNC basketball family, and our paths intersected at banquets and games and athletic functions. When my husband and I attended one of her annual family days or awards banquets, as soon as she spotted us, she would push her way through her adoring fans to thank us personally for coming. Then she would publicly acknowledge us from the platform. She made us feel special.

But the first time I remember having a lengthy, in-depth, one-on-one conversation with Sylvia was when we met for lunch years ago. Just the two of us. I came away from that incredible visit and told my husband, "I have just spent two hours with a woman who has absolutely no hang-ups. No baggage. And who loves life." From that moment forward, I wanted to get to know her better. I count it one of God's highest honors and blessings to be considered her friend.

As Sylvia's friend, I have spoken to hundreds of people gathered for a picnic on the front lawn of her home—with the sound system cranked up so her neighbors could hear. I have given the invocation before her formal dinners and banquets, with her whispered encouragement in the politically correct atmosphere, "You go for it, girl." I have sat with my husband on her team's bench as we were named honorary coaches.

I have preached from the pulpit in her church with her team and their families seated before me. I have stood on center court with her as she presented a large, personal donation to the Kay Yow Cancer Fund.

But perhaps one of the highlights of our relationship was when I invited Sylvia, her husband Sammy, and her son Van to come up to my father's house for a visit. I expected them to arrive, greet my father, evangelist Billy Graham, say a few things, take a few pictures, and leave. Instead, Sammy pulled out his guitar, asked Daddy for hymns he might like to sing, and for about thirty minutes we all sang one hymn after another! They hadn't come to take *from* my father; they had come to minister blessing *to* him.

And that's Sylvia Hatchell. She is a giver. Not a taker. In this book she will give you the challenge and the courage to discover your inner strength when you too are blindsided by life. Read it. Then pass it on.

- INTRODUCTION -

Heading into the 2013 season, my twenty-eighth at the helm of the University of North Carolina Tar Heels women's basketball program, I had the strangest of dreams. I dreamt that I was sitting in the stands at Carmichael Arena watching my team play on the court below. When I awoke in the morning, I could remember it vividly, and I shared intricate details of my dream with my husband, Sammy. I asked him, "Why in the world would I be sitting in the stands watching my team play?"

Of course, dreams are just dreams. I never took it seriously. After all, it didn't make sense. I was on top of the basketball world professionally at the time. Our program was on the rise.

Merely months later, however, I would learn that the dream was a glimpse into reality. Oddly, I was almost finished writing a memoir around this time, reflecting on my four decades of coaching, but it was suddenly as if none of that mattered. My story was beginning anew.

Looking back, I can see that my story began with that confusing dream, and it now makes perfect sense...

- Chapter 1 -
TOP OF THE WORLD

"I don't look at this moment as a defining end to my relationship with the game of basketball. It's simply a continuation of something that I started a long time ago."
~Michael Jordan, UNC Class of 1986, Naismith Memorial Basketball Hall of Fame induction speech

It was not an easy task when I first started coaching the women's basketball team at the University of North Carolina. In fact, the women's basketball program had arguably never been in worse condition than in my first half-decade here.

UNC athletic director John Swofford hired me after the Francis Marion team that I had been coaching for eleven years won an NAIA National Championship in 1986. My first season coaching the Tar Heels went okay. We advanced to the second round of the NCAA tournament, but then several of our players graduated. The 1987 season was supposed to be my big recruiting year, but I invested much of my time working with the USA women's basketball team in the wake of head coach Kay Yow's breast cancer diagnosis, preparing the team for the 1988 Olympics in Seoul, South Korea. Our next four seasons at UNC were dreadful. In four years, we posted a combined 45–68 record—four straight losing seasons.

Around this time, when the program was in its depths, a journalist from the *Herald-Sun* in Durham wrote a story titled "Black Cloud in Blue Heaven" about how the program was struggling. I really felt like he was trying to get me fired. It was as if he was on a witch-hunt or something. I still have the story today. I read it from time to time to remind myself that tough times don't last but tough people do.

I found it futile to grow angry with the journalist or become bitter about people's potential perceptions of me—actions like that just wear away at your personal happiness. Instead, I ended up befriending the journalist. I even took him to church with me at one point. I decided I'd try to make him my best friend. My mother always told me: "Kill them with kindness." I couldn't control what others said about me, but I could control the way I reacted to what they said. I could control my work ethic and my mentality. Everything else was out of my hands.

Seven years later, after an NCAA championship and two Sweet Sixteen appearances, that same journalist wrote a story titled "Born to Coach"—the exact opposite of the article he had written more than a half-decade before.

I share this story often with others, not to highlight my coaching abilities or the progression of the program but because I think it demonstrates how vital it is for us, in our daily lives, to turn negativity into something positive, to find the good in the bad, to undergo personal transformation in adversity, and to allow challenges to enhance the story God is authoring in our lives.

∽

I will not go into many details about my coaching career in this book, but I will say that as I entered 2013, I felt as if I was on top of the coaching world. I recall some of my closest friends telling me at the start of 2013 that it was going to be a year I would always remember. It certainly began that way.

In February, I earned my nine hundredth victory as a head coach—an 80–52 win on the road against Boston College in ACC play. It was a special moment. UNC had even surprised me by flying Sammy, my husband, and our son, Van, to Boston for the game. After the victory, caps with "900 Wins" plastered on the front were passed out to our players and coaches. The Boston College athletics department even provided a cake and some flowers for our celebration.

Their participation speaks volumes about the tight-knit fraternity of coaches in our profession; we always want to beat each other on the court, but when the game is over, we are colleagues who work together to improve the game of women's basketball, even to the point of providing cake and flowers to applaud a milestone. I was humbled on so many levels that day and was thankful to be doing what I was most passionate about in my life: coaching and encouraging young people at an institution I loved, the University of North Carolina. I was overwhelmed with gratitude.

One week later, things got even better when I received a call from the Naismith Memorial Basketball Hall of Fame making me aware that I had been nominated for the upcoming induction class. This did not ensure my induction. After a candidate's name is submitted for consideration, members of the Hall of Fame vote to reject or validate a nominee. Regardless, it was beyond humbling that I was even being considered for such a distinguished honor, to be included among such a prestigious circle of basketball legends. The announcement wouldn't be made until April, so I pressed on with our season.

Our team performed well, finishing the regular season with a 26–5 record and a 14–4 record in ACC play, our best record in the ACC since our 14–0 undefeated conference record in the 2007–08 season five years earlier. In the postseason we advanced to the ACC Championship but fell to Duke; in the NCAA tournament we advanced to the second round but lost to Delaware. After not even making the tournament the year before, it was a solid year for us, a step in the right direction.

What's more is that I knew we had the No. 1-ranked recruiting class coming in the next season. This was primarily because of May 4, 2012, the best recruiting day in the history of UNC women's basketball, when four top-tiered players who played on the USA basketball team together—Diamond DeShields, Alisha Gray, Stephanie Mavunga, and Jessica Washington—all made a pact to come to UNC. I was ecstatic. It was yet another reason why 2013 was going to be one for the record books.

And it continued to get better…

∽

It was a typical spring afternoon in Chapel Hill, North Carolina, and I had just finished working out with my physical trainer. I was picking up a salad at a nearby grocery store when my phone rang—it was a number that I did not recognize. I answered it anyway. That's when I heard a voice say, "Sylvia, this is John Doleva. It's my pleasure to inform you that you have been selected for enshrinement in the Naismith Memorial Basketball Hall of Fame."

Though I had dreamt of this moment, I was utterly shocked when it actually happened. I was numb. I couldn't move. Looking back, I hope that I had the good manners to say "Thank you" to Mr. Doleva, the president and CEO of the Hall of Fame, but I don't remember if I did. After the call, I just sat there in the parking lot of the grocery store. I was thrilled, but I did not trust myself to drive. For several minutes I sat there and thought that I might have to call my assistant and ask her to drive me back to campus. It doesn't get any better than the Naismith Memorial Basketball Hall of Fame.

I would be entering the Hall of Fame with the late Roger Brown, a four-time ABA All-Star and three-time ABA champion; former President of USA Basketball Russ Granik; six-time NBA All-Star Richie Guerin; the late Edwin Bancroft Henderson, known as the "Father of Black Basketball"; four-time NBA All-Star Bernard King; former University of Houston head coach Guy V. Lewis, who led Phi Slama Jama to five NCAA Final Fours; nine-time NBA All-Star Gary Payton; two-time NCAA champion Rick Pitino; Oscar Daniel Bezerra Schmidt, the all-time leading scorer in Olympic basketball history; Dawn Staley, a three-time Olympian who was voted by fans as one of the top fifteen players in WNBA history; and the late Jerry Tarkanian, 1990 NCAA champion and four-time National Coach of the Year. Who was I to be a part of an induction class as prestigious as this?

I was told that our acceptance as inductees into the 2013 Naismith Class would be made public at halftime of the NCAA men's basketball championship game that following Monday in Atlanta. In the meantime, I couldn't tell anyone about the news I had received besides my family and the coaching staff. That's the hardest secret I've ever had to keep! I was bursting with joy from within!

And to think that this was only the start of an unbelievable year.

One thing about the people at the Naismith Memorial Basketball Hall of Fame is that they make you feel like royalty.

On Sunday night, the day before the 2013 NCAA men's basketball national championship game between the University of Louisville and the University of Michigan, we were treated to a dinner at Morton's, a steakhouse in downtown Atlanta. It was our first time together as a Hall of Fame class. At the dinner, we were asked to share where we were and what we were doing when we received the phone call from Mr. Doleva about our enshrinement. People found it humorous that I was so emotional after the call that I was hesitant to drive a mile or so back to campus from the grocery store parking lot.

The next morning at a press conference with all the inductees, I remember being amazed that Louisville head coach Rick Pitino was in attendance even though his team was playing in the national championship game that evening. The fact that he was there is a great example of how much the Naismith means to people in the basketball world.

The festivities continued that evening when the 2013 class once more came together and watched the national championship game from a skybox at the Georgia Dome. At halftime we were honored in front of the crowd of seventy-five thousand people. That moment, standing on the court with such an elite group of inductees, is one that I will never forget.

In September, we would be honored at the Naismith Memorial Basketball Hall of Fame in Springfield, Massachusetts, and in October I would begin coaching a team that had gone 29–7 the year before and would be joined by the No. 1 recruiting class in the country.

∽

The offseason was pretty typical, but there were a couple interesting situations that might be worth mentioning, beginning with my annual physical before the start of the fall semester.

My physical was scheduled for the Thursday before Labor Day weekend; I felt great and was confident the results would reveal that I was in excellent health. I was in the best shape of my life and was working out with a personal trainer twice a week. Never had I felt better. I was strong as an ox.

When I arrived at my physical, the physician's assistant told me that health insurance had changed and that I no longer had to get a blood test. However, in 2000, I had a scare with the possibility of ovarian cancer, so since that time, I have always requested to have a CA 125 blood test performed, a test that helps detect cancer. I wasn't going to stop just because my health insurance no longer covered it.

They completed my physical, and on Thursday night I drove from Chapel Hill to our beach house in North Myrtle Beach, South Carolina. Labor Day weekend is always something I look forward to; it gives Sammy and me a little time together before basketball season kicks into full gear. My husband coaches too and is the all-time winningest coach at Meredith College; he also helped lead Shaw University to the 2011–12 NCAA Division II national title. Needless to say, the last two years had been a whirlwind for both of us.

Down in North Myrtle, Sammy and I usually got together with our special beach friends for cookouts and drop by the O.D. Pavilion, Fat Harold's, and other shag clubs in the evenings to go dancing. I love the beach, and I love shag dancing—it's great exercise, fun music, and our friends whom we go with are excellent, down-to-earth people.

On Friday morning, I received a call from the doctor's office where I had gotten my physical. The nurse told me they had received the results from my blood work and were concerned because my white cell count was low. It was 1.3.

"What's it supposed to be?" I asked.

"Over 4.0," she replied.

"So what does this mean?" I asked.

"Well," she said, "you may have a viral infection or some kind of autoimmune thing going on, but we would like you to see a hematologist today, if possible."

I told her that I was at the beach and wouldn't be returning until Monday.

"We will set something up for Tuesday," she said. "In the meantime, don't be around anyone who is sick, don't be shaking hands with people, don't eat any raw fruits or vegetables, and avoid salad bars or anything like that."

Whatever it was that I had, it sounded like it had the potential to be somewhat serious if I had to be that cautious. Anyway, that was how my Labor Day weekend began.

On Saturday night, Sammy and I went to an annual shrimp festival, the Labor Day Forest Gump Shrimp Bunch, with our friends—former coaches, UNC alumni, shaggers, and our wonderful beach friends—an event that has become a tradition for all of us over the years. After the shrimp festival, however, I tried to be careful and mostly lay low the rest of the weekend, just as the nurse had recommended.

I went to my appointment with the hematologist on Tuesday, and they got my blood work back on Wednesday. I was scheduled to fly to Springfield, Massachusetts, to be inducted into the Hall of Fame on Thursday, so I really hoped they wouldn't find anything seriously wrong—that would have been horrible timing.

Fortunately, they didn't find anything serious.

Everything was okay.

Praise God.

"You either have an autoimmune disease or a viral infection," the hematologist said. "We'll give it a couple weeks, but your white blood cell count should come back up. We'll do another blood test in a couple weeks."

Considering how much I was traveling and spending time with college kids, picking up a viral infection was very plausible. The good news was that I didn't have any symptoms, and I believed I was as healthy as could be. My immune system would surely fight off whatever it was that I had. Still, the whole scenario was quite the scare before entering arguably the biggest weekend of my life.

"In the meantime," said the hematologist before hanging up the phone, "stay away from people who are sick. Oh yeah, and don't be shaking hands."

The thought of not shaking any hands at the Naismith Hall of Fame, the epicenter of the basketball world, was a comical one, so I bluntly told the hematologist that there was no possible way I would be able to go the duration of the weekend without shaking any hands. In fact, I would be shaking more hands than I ever had before. When I explained to him where I was going, he laughed and understood, but he did recommend that I wear a mask on my flight. I felt a little foolish, but I did.

∽

The Naismith was unbelievable. The place was flowing with such a remarkable sense of community, spirit of oneness, and genuine love for the game of basketball. It is the ultimate experience for a coach or a player. All the "Who's Who" in the basketball world were there—

people like UCLA legend Bill Walton, three-time NBA MVP Larry Bird, five-time NBA champion Magic Johnson, Harlem Globetrotters star Meadowlark Lemon...I could go on and on.

After numerous press conferences and interviews on Thursday, Friday was filled with activities. The kind people at the Naismith made us inductees feel like the most important people on the planet. We received our rings at a huge ceremony on Friday night and our Hall of Fame jackets at a press conference on Saturday, and we attended a private dinner that evening at which all the members of the Naismith were present. As I had predicted, I shook plenty of hands—believe me.

At the private dinner, there were no media or cameras, so it wasn't like anyone was trying to outdo anyone else or make a business move. For once, in a room full of players and coaches, there was little competition. Everyone was there simply because of his or her love and appreciation for the game of basketball. The only other place where I have felt that sense of oneness within the basketball community was at Dean Smith's private funeral in 2015.

Sunday was the official induction, and it was broadcasted live on national television. When I had been initially notified of my induction months before, the Naismith folks told me to give them a list of people that I wanted to invite to the official ceremony. No one told me to limit the length of my list, so I invited everyone who I thought might want to travel to Massachusetts that weekend and celebrate with me. My list topped seventeen hundred, and the folks at the Naismith told me I had invited more people than anyone in the history of the event. It might just seem like a funny story, but I truly wanted everyone I knew to be a part of the celebration; there was no way I could have made it this far in my coaching career without the loving support of my family, friends, staff, players, mentors, and all those who helped me along the way. In the end, I narrowed my list down; about two hundred people were there to celebrate with me in Springfield.

The entire weekend was a dream come true, the most extraordinary weekend of my life. Though I am not one who usually looks back at the past and reflects—as I am usually pressing forward toward new goals—I was forced to reflect that weekend. It is always humbling to reflect on what God has done in your life. Fellow coaches of the women's game like Kay Yow, Pat Summitt, C. Vivian Stringer, Jody Conradt, Tara VanDerveer, Sue Gunter, Billie Moore, and Margaret Wade had made it into the Naismith, and I was honored just to be a part of such an elite list.

When I returned to Chapel Hill on Monday, I began to mentally transition into the upcoming season. The Naismith was great; but now there was work to do. Recruiting season was beginning, and, with the No. 1-ranked recruiting class joining a team that was already on the up and up, I wanted to keep building for the future.

The way 2013 was going, I believed that the upcoming season might be one where North Carolina women's basketball made a statement on the national scale.

It was our time.

- Chapter 2 -
YEAR TO REMEMBER

"There are always new, grander challenges to confront, and a true winner will embrace each one."
~Mia Hamm, UNC Class of 1993, U.S. women's national soccer team

The Monday after the Naismith festivities was the first day of recruiting for Division I coaches. It was time to get rolling. There was work to do.

Sammy and I got home at around eleven thirty in the morning, and I had time to eat lunch and change my clothes before heading to the Raleigh airport, as my assistant coaches and I had a recruiting visit scheduled with the No. 1 high school player in the country in Columbia, South Carolina. From there, we flew to Maryland for another recruiting visit.

When I gave my presentation to the recruit in Maryland, I noticed that my throat was feeling slightly sore. By the time we got back on the university plane that evening, my throat was really sore. The initial recruiting period involves flying all over the country for visits; although I do a lot of talking and the travel is draining, it is never debilitating. We returned to Chapel Hill.

Before flying out to Atlanta to visit two more recruits the next day, I called one of my doctor friends, Dr. Rick Pillsbury, the head of Ear, Nose & Throat at UNC, and told him that my throat was sore and that I needed him to check me for strep throat before I went on any more recruiting visits. That'd be one way to scare off recruits: go to their homes and give them and their families strep throat!

Dr. Pillsbury—who had always been a huge supporter of women's basketball at UNC and had arguably saved the life of a former player of mine, Jessica Breland, by discovering her Hodgkin's lymphoma in 2009—told me to come on over.

After evaluating my throat, he said that my lymph glands were swollen. I told him about my low white blood cell count, and he arranged for me to see a doctor at the UNC Infectious Disease Clinic the next day. They confirmed that I probably had an autoimmune disorder or viral infection.

I was given a prescription for some medication to help my throat, and we hopped on our flight to Atlanta.

∽

The medication helped, and I continued recruiting until the end of September. Before I knew it, October was upon me, and it was time to start basketball practice. I was drained from the recruiting period—more tired than usual—but I couldn't wait to dive into the season.

The first week of October, I remember sitting on a panel at a media luncheon hosted by our local television personality, Debra Morgan from WRAL, next to North Carolina State head coach Wes Moore, Duke head coach Joanne McCallie, and North Carolina Central head coach Vanessa Taylor. Though all the coaches were excited about the upcoming season, no one could have been more enthusiastic than I was. I typically try not to get too high or too low in my emotions when it comes to my approach to our competition, but as typical as my answers might have sounded that day at the media luncheon, deep down I was confident that the 2013–14 UNC season was going to be special. Really special.

∽

When I returned from the luncheon, my hematologist called and informed me that my white blood cell count in my follow-up blood test was still just as low as before.

I decided to take matters into my own hands. I still did not feel very well, which was weird for me. I needed to get to the bottom of my medical situation before the season began. (We coaches tend to take control when we aren't getting the results we desire.)

I called a friend, Debbie Dibert, the director of development at UNC Lineberger Cancer Center, and asked her to put me in touch with someone to perform a bone marrow biopsy. I understand that it sounds odd for me to directly call a hospital administrator and ask her to find someone to perform a specific medical procedure, but I was desperate to figure out what was going on with my body. It was not normal. I wanted to put the illness behind me and feel like myself again. Since I had done a lot of fundraising with Lineberger over the years, they were happy to help me any way they could.

On Friday morning I went to Lineberger for a bone marrow biopsy. I had a hole drilled into my hip, got bone marrow removed, and was back on the court for practice at Carmichael Arena with my team that afternoon.

∽

That evening, I had plans with one of my good friends, Dianne Glover, a registered nurse and research program manager at UNC Vascular Surgery. Sammy was working a basketball clinic at East Carolina University, so Dianne and I decided that we were going to have a casual "girls' night," one of my favorite things to do. She was going to come over and we were simply going to listen to music and organize my house. My friends joke with me that "organizing my house" simply means moving all my stuff from one place to another since I have a hard time throwing things away. And I have a lot of stuff.

At around eight thirty in the evening, as Dianne was helping me sort through some of my clutter while blasting an "On the Beach with Charlie Brown" CD, my favorite shag music, I received a call on my landline phone.

"Hello," I said, while walking into the next room and closing the door to the blasting music.

"Hi, can I speak to Mrs. Hatchell please?" said the voice on the other end.

I thought it was a solicitor, so I said, "I'm sorry, she's not here right now; can I take a message?"

"Okay, this is Dr. Peter Voorhees from the Lineberger Cancer Center—"

"Dr. Voorhees, it's me," I interrupted. "I'm sorry, I thought you were a solicitor."

After some small talk, Dr. Voorhees cut straight to the chase.

"Coach Hatchell," he said, "we have received the preliminary results from your bone marrow biopsy this afternoon, and it revealed that you have acute myeloid leukemia."

To be honest, I had no idea what this meant exactly. I knew that "leukemia" was a heavy word, but I was clueless as to what this would entail for me. I obviously knew it was more serious than a viral infection or autoimmune illness—this was cancer, after all—but I didn't know how serious.

"It's treatable and it's curable," he continued, "but we've got to get you in here and get control of this."

"When do you need me to come in?" I asked.

"Tomorrow, Coach," he said. "This is serious."

When he said "tomorrow," I was in disbelief. I had too much going on in the upcoming week to check into a hospital.

"Tomorrow is Saturday," I said.

"Coach, this is serious," he repeated.

Dr. Voorhees went on to tell me that I would be in the hospital for at least a month. A month? What was happening?

A few minutes later, our conversation came to an end. I hung up and walked back into the bedroom. I was in a daze. Utterly shocked.

"Dianne," I said, "I have acute myeloid leukemia."

Almost immediately Dianne broke down and started to cry. Because she was a nurse, I think she knew how serious it was to have AML for a woman my age. Though I didn't know it then, I now understand that the five-year overall survival rate at the time was around twenty-five percent. It was even more difficult for people above the age of sixty. I was sixty-one.

Dianne walked toward me and we embraced, there in my bedroom. She cried on my shoulder. I think I was too shocked to feel anything at all.

- Chapter 3 -
REALITY

*"In Sleep we lie all naked and alone, in Sleep we are united at
the heart of night and darkness, and we are strange and beautiful
asleep; for we are dying the darkness and we know no death."*
~Thomas Wolfe (1900–1938), UNC Class of 1920, novelist

At the time I do not think I realized that my life had dramatically
changed in a matter of seconds—with one phone call. That first night, I
was too shocked to comprehend my new reality. Maybe even in denial.
Did I really have cancer?

The year was going too well for something like cancer to strike. Nine
hundred wins, the Naismith, a top-ranked recruiting class. Not now.
Not this year. Plus, I was too busy for something like that to happen.
The next week was fall break. My friends and I were looking forward
to spending some time at my log-cabin home in Black Mountain,
North Carolina. On Tuesday night I was scheduled to do a promo with
country artist and bluegrass singer Ricky Skaggs for Carson-Newman
University in Jefferson City, Tennessee, where I went to school. On
Thursday I was supposed to ride horses for a promo at the Biltmore
House in Asheville, North Carolina. I was moving one hundred miles
per hour, as I usually did around this time of year. And now I was just
supposed to let my life come to a screeching halt? When Dr. Voorhees
first delivered the news to me, I remember asking him, "Don't you have
a pill or something that you can give me?"

What did all this mean—*acute myeloid leukemia?*

I didn't tell many people that night about my diagnosis. The only people who knew anything at all were those at Lineberger and Dianne. I called Sammy that evening, but I did not tell him that I had leukemia. I didn't want him to be worried as he drove back from his coaching clinic at East Carolina. So I told him that I had a blood disease. And, though I was loathe to ask him to come back early from his coaching clinic, I told him that I would need him to take me to the hospital on Saturday afternoon. I also called Van, our only child, and told him that I needed to see him on Saturday around lunchtime to talk about a few things, but I didn't tell him I'd be checking into the hospital the very next day. I also contacted my staff and asked them to meet at my house at ten o'clock in the morning.

What was especially odd that evening was that Dianne and I went from casually organizing my bedroom closet and listening to beach music to all of a sudden packing a suitcase for my upcoming month-long hospital stay. How exactly are you supposed to go about packing when you are going to be gone for a month?

Dianne packed a lot of pajamas for me. I just packed tons of gym clothes.

At one point we took a break, and I remember sitting on the floor in my bedroom next to my suitcase; Dianne was sitting on a nearby couch. We began talking about God and faith and how it related to a broken moment like this. Dianne prayed for me. I didn't know what was going on, but I believed God had a plan for my life.

Dianne spent the night at my house. She did not want me to be alone.

∽

The next morning, after a surprisingly decent night of sleep, I received a call from Dr. Shelley Earp, director of UNC Cancer Care and Lineberger Cancer Center. I have a long history with Lineberger (which I will explain later in this chapter), and that is why I have deep, personal friendships with so many people who work there.

He left a message on my cell phone and said, "Coach, Shelley Earp here. I'm in New York at a conference. I'm so sorry about your diagnosis, and I wish I could be with you there today to put my arms around you and give you a hug when you come in. But with your fighting spirit and our expert doctors in cancer care and your competitive mentality, we're going to beat this thing. After all these years that you've been giving to Lineberger and doing things for us, now it's our time to take care of you."

It was beginning to settle in.

Early in the morning, I gave a call to my mentor Anne Graham Lotz, the daughter of Reverend Billy Graham. Anne has been a spiritual mentor to me for a long time. Our conversations have always given me great perspective and have fueled me with life-giving truth. When Anne answered the phone, she was on her way up to Norfolk, Virginia, to speak. She was devastated when I delivered the news to her.

"We haven't put anything out to the media yet," I told her.

"Okay," she said, "I will call my dad and have him pray for you, but I won't tell anyone else until it is made public."

She called me three times throughout the course of the day and told me that she and her father were praying.

∽

Around ten o'clock in the morning, members of my staff began to arrive at my house. My dear friend and longtime personal assistant, Jane High, later told me that she realized that our meeting was going to be a serious one when she saw other staff members arriving as well. She had thought she was simply meeting with me to do some scheduling and organizing for the coming month, as she often did. I guess we still were, just not in the fashion she expected. Also, when Jane arrived, Dianne was just leaving and Jane noticed tear stains on her face as they made eye contact on the porch. Dianne did not say anything to Jane; she simply shook her head in disbelief.

A few of our coaches were out of town that day. Telling them would have to wait. But Andrew Calder, who had been my assistant since I took the head coaching job at Chapel Hill in 1986, was there. So was Tracey Williams, who had coached alongside me for a decade and a half.

Jane, Andrew, and Tracey met with me for an hour, there in my living room. The three of them sat on a couch, and I stood in front of them and straightforwardly told them, "I got a diagnosis, and it's not good. It's acute myeloid leukemia. I'm going to be out for a while, and we need to make arrangements. Coach Calder, you are going to have to take over for me while I'm out."

Everyone was, as expected, shocked.

"I'll be checking in to the hospital today at three o'clock," I told them. "They are putting my port in today, and I will begin chemotherapy tomorrow."

I tried to be strong, and I could tell they were trying to be strong, too. But it was a confusing moment for them, I'm sure. Cancer not only affected my life; it affected theirs. Their roles would drastically change.

I noticed some tears welling up in their eyes.

In the silence, Jane said, "May I pray?"

"Sure," I said, "thank you."

After a pause, she began. "Lord, guide us through all this," she prayed quietly. "You know the steps that we need to take. You know the strength that we all need. Guide us through that, and show us where You can use us, Lord. Help us to glorify You in all that we do. Most of all, please be with Coach Hatchell. Give her strength to handle this bout with cancer. We know that You have a plan."

When our meeting came to an end, I gave them all hugs. When I embraced Andrew, he broke down. Like a brother and sister, we had been through a lot together and would do anything for each other. He had been extremely loyal to me for over thirty years. Still, I had never seen him like that before. The dam in the room seemed to break, because once Andrew started to bawl, so did the others.

It had yet to settle in for me. But it had apparently settled in for them.

∽

After my staff left, Van arrived.

When I told Van, he was stunned but replied, "We'll beat this, Mama. I know you will."

Sammy arrived later that afternoon.

Whereas I am more of an optimist, Sammy is more of a realist who sometimes leans toward pessimism. I told him that I needed him to be positive and refrain from overreacting throughout this process, whatever that process entailed, though overreacting was certainly an understandable reaction considering the apparent heaviness.

I told them both, "Guys, I have to do this, and I need both of you to take care of things for me around the house while I'm gone."

Though I had an idea that my life was about to drastically change, I didn't want theirs to change all that much, from their day-to-day routines to their emotional health. That was important to me. I wanted them to keep living. This was my fight. What would help my emotional well-being the most would be if those who were closest to me, specifically my husband and son, continued to live normally and press on with their lives.

The three of us, along with my niece Amanda who was living at our house, left for the hospital at two thirty in the afternoon.

It was time to check in.

∽

I had been to the UNC Lineberger Comprehensive Cancer Center hundreds of times. For more than two decades, I had been doing anything I could to support them because I believed in what they did. I visited often.

My first encounter with Lineberger was in the spring of 2000. Just days before I was scheduled to take my team to Australia, my doctors told me that there was a possibility that I had ovarian cancer. I told no one, not even my husband, and flew off to Australia with my team. When I returned to Chapel Hill, I told Sammy about the prognosis, went through a battery of more tests, and eventually checked into the hospital for surgery. Though it seemed pretty certain that I had ovarian cancer, it was discovered that I actually had benign tumors and a severe case of endometriosis. I was lucky, but this initial encounter with a serious illness gave me a glimpse into the Lineberger Cancer Center, where I learned about the excellent work that they did and about how much they genuinely cared about their patients.

I remember thinking to myself at the time: *There must be a reason why God wants me to know about the good work these people do. How can I be a part of what they are doing? How can I help?*

So I became an enthusiastic fundraiser for the Lineberger Cancer Center.

Throughout the 2000–01 season, I personally donated five dollars for every women's basketball season ticket sold at Carmichael. And over the years I have enjoyed coming up with other innovative fundraising techniques, playing a small part in helping meet the needs at Lineberger.

Another one of these fundraising ideas came through my family's two-hundred-acre property in Black Mountain. When we purchased the property in 2000, I was told that I could probably profit from the cluster of blueberry bushes that were planted near the road on our property. I knew the folks in the community frequently stopped by to pick some blueberries from our little blueberry patch, but I had no intention of becoming a blueberry farmer. However, at the time, I was also learning about the benefits of blueberries as an antioxidant and how they might be considered a "superfood" when it came to cancer prevention. I thought to myself: *Here is God once again opening up a door for me to help Lineberger.*

I decided to clean up the blueberry patch and plant more bushes. One day Sammy and I nailed a sign to the big oak tree next to patch that read:

Lineberger Cancer Center Blueberries Patch
Honor System
Mail checks to PO Box 2411
Chapel Hill, NC 27514

Over the years the blueberry patch has grown to over two hundred fifty bushes, and people continue to send very generous donations to the Lineberger Cancer Center. I think the greatest benefit, honestly, has been the exposure that the blueberry patch has brought to Lineberger. The good people at Lineberger don't spend much money on marketing because they believe that most of the money they raise should go toward research so they can save more lives. There have been many patients who have heard about Lineberger through the blueberry patch; one even went on to become the keynote speaker at one of their functions.

All that is to say that it was much different walking through the doors of the hospital this time around. No longer was I walking into that place asking how I could help them as a donor, business partner, and friend. No longer was I visiting the schoolroom in the children's cancer wing that I had sponsored in honor of Jessica Breland, whose life had been saved by Dr. Pillsbury. Now I was walking into that place dependent on *them* to save *my* life. It felt kind of backwards, honestly. I'm not sure if it really registered that day, that fateful Saturday.

I had to check in at the women's hospital wing because of how the cancer center operates on weekends, so Sammy pulled up beneath the five-pillared overhang on the southeast side of the building and dropped me off. After getting checked in, we walked down the hallway and into a well-lit, open, circular atrium, with its wall of glass windows and wood-colored paneling. There, I finished the check-in process before eventually taking the elevator to the fourth floor and into a spacious hallway overlooking the entire medical section of campus. This side of the hospital, facing campus, was shaped like a gigantic C. *C as in Carolina.*

Whether I realized it at the time or not, October 12, 2013 would mark the first day of fighting for my life.

I turned left, walked through a door, and into a section of the hospital that would be my home for at least the next month—the front lines of my fight. What's interesting is that I had just been to this fourth-floor wing merely two months before to visit a friend of mine, Alisha Larkins Scudder, who had been diagnosed with an aggressive form of breast cancer that had spread to her brain. Alisha and I had grown up in Gastonia together and had attended Unity Baptist Church in our youth, spending many summers at South Mountain Baptist Camp and other church functions. She was a bundle of energy who was always selflessly doing things for other people.

When she was blindsided by cancer, she called me because she had nowhere to turn. I connected her with Lineberger, and she stayed at my house during her treatments. The doctors and nurses prolonged her life but also saw the cancer viciously spread after cutting open her spine during surgery. Following that operation, things turned south. I remember her telling me during the summer, in her weakest moments, that she only hoped that she would live through November for the birth of her grandchild. When her son and his wife were in town that August, I had it arranged for a friend of mine, Dr. Harry Stafford, our team physician, to take a portable ultrasound into Alisha's room one Tuesday afternoon while her son and daughter-in-law were visiting the hospital—so then she could see her grandchild on a screen. Unfortunately, Alisha went into a coma on Tuesday morning, hours before the scheduled ultrasound. She never woke up, which was very sad for the family.

⚭

With the help of Dr. Voorhees, who would be the doctor handling my case, I was able to comprehend more about acute myeloid leukemia that day at the hospital. Basically, acute myeloid leukemia (AML) is a cancer of the blood and bone marrow in which the bone marrow produces abnormal myeloblasts that do not become healthy white blood cells. This explained why my white blood cell count was low. What's important to know is that AML is an aggressive type of cancer that can quickly get worse if it's not treated. That's why there was no delaying my arrival at the hospital. Chemotherapy awaited me.

I respected Dr. Voorhees from the get-go. He was honest with me. He did not sugarcoat things. He was very personable and easy to talk to, but at the same time, he did not try to dance around some of the harsh realities associated with my diagnosis. Because he was blunt and truthful with me in the dismal times, I knew that I would be able to trust him when good news might arise in the future.

Though I was learning more about AML that day, I chose not to sift through any of the survival statistics or anything like that. There were books and packets available at Lineberger where I could have learned some of those specifics, but I decided that none of that could possibly lead to anything positive in my mind or my thinking.

⚭

After filling out some paperwork and going through a number of tests in preparation for my treatments, I continued to make arrangements for the coming week. I wasn't looking forward to Sunday. Not only would chemo begin, which was unknown territory for me, but even worse, I would also have to deliver the news about my diagnosis to my players. They had chosen North Carolina to play for me, and now I had to break the news to them that I wouldn't be able to coach them for the unforeseeable future.

In my four decades of coaching, I had experienced just about everything. I had seen players get serious illnesses and guided them and their families through that difficult process. I had seen players lose parents and best friends and siblings. But this, telling them that *I* had cancer, was uncharted territory.

After talking to my staff on Saturday, we decided that the assistant coaches would take the players over to Lineberger on Sunday afternoon so I could talk to them. The players had no idea that I was in the hospital. It wasn't out of the ordinary to take them over to Lineberger because we would often volunteer over there; I was passionate about helping this vital cancer center any way we could, and we would often spend time encouraging some of the patients. But this time, I was not looking forward to being the patient they visited. I did not want to throw this type of news upon them. I did not want Sunday to come.

On Saturday I had my assistant call my friends who were planning on joining me at my cabin in Black Mountain that week and tell them that they were still welcome to spend a few days there but that I would not be able to be there. My friend Jackie Koss, who I had formed a friendship with during the seventies and early eighties while working at Pat Summitt's basketball camps, was the first to call and ask, "What's wrong?"

Truth is, I did not yet feel comfortable with anyone knowing about my disease, even my closest friends, but Jackie is a genuine, no-nonsense gal, and I knew I could not put her off. Plus, she was a nurse practitioner in oncology at Vanderbilt University, so I knew she would understand. I told her, "I have leukemia, and I'm beginning my treatments tomorrow."

"I'll see you in the morning," she told me.

She decided that she would drive all night from Manchester, Tennessee, just south of Nashville.

∽

As darkness fell upon Chapel Hill, I eventually sent Van and Sammy home, and for the first time, I began to contemplate my strange reality while lying in bed in the lonely solitude of my hospital room. It was hard for me not to get up and walk out of that place. It all felt like a bad dream.

I was just inducted into the Naismith Hall of Fame. What in the world am I doing here in the hospital?

I am a control freak. I like to have every single day planned out down to the very last minute. All of a sudden, I didn't even know, or understand, what the next day entailed. I kept thinking about my team and the joyful anticipation I had experienced as the season approached. The season was about to begin, and suddenly it was the most removed thing from my mind. For the first time in four decades, basketball was forced to take a back seat.

Reality began to sink in. It was the longest of nights.

I cried myself to sleep.

- Chapter 4 -
HOLD THE ROPE

"When you die, that does not mean that you lose to cancer. You beat cancer by how you live, why you live, and the manner in which you live."
~Stuart Scott (1965–2015), UNC Class of 1987, ESPN sportscaster who received the Jimmy V Award prior to his death from cancer

When I awoke, Jackie Koss was standing at my bedside. She had made the ten-hour drive through the night to Chapel Hill. I was humbled. After the worst night of my life, I was greeted in the morning by one of my best friends.

"I'm here for the week," she told me.

As I went through the day, I realized how much of a godsend it was to have Jackie there with me. As an oncology nurse practitioner, Jackie spoke the language of the cancer doctors, and she was able to help me understand the medical jargon. Though my world was spinning, she was able to walk me through an understanding of the procedures and help me mentally prepare for what was to come. This was new territory for me. As a former coach, she was also able to communicate to the doctors how important it was for me to be completely candid about my diagnosis and treatment to my team and the media.

That morning, doctors inserted a double port in my chest.

They told me that I would begin chemotherapy after I talked to my team that evening.

∽

The clock in my hospital room read 4:00 PM.

That meant that my team was currently meeting at Carmichael Arena for practice. Soon, however, the assistant coaches would be taking them over to the conference room at the cancer center.

My staff was careful not to disclose my whereabouts to the players. Because everything had happened so quickly, it was important that they heard it straight from me, the source. After all, I had seen them at practice on Friday afternoon; now I had a double port in my chest and a mask over my face. How quickly things had changed!

It was important that we were clear with them about my status and the journey ahead. We did not want them to be uncertain about anything or feel as if we were keeping them in the dark; they deserved clarity. And we did not want them talking with others about my diagnosis. Not yet. We had to keep all of this in-house for now.

The players were told to bring along our team's knotted rope to encourage a "cancer patient." They just didn't know that I was the patient. This rope was part of a tradition that we began a few years before, where we would all hold the strong cord of twisted blue and white cloth when someone was going through a tough time. This demonstrated unity—that we would hold the rope for the hurting individual while he or she was going through a trial. This could be someone in our program or someone outside of the program.

Not long past four o'clock, I was made aware that the girls were about to be ushered into the ground-floor conference room. I strapped a mask over my face to protect myself from any germs. Perhaps even more difficult than bearing this horrible news to them was the fact that I would not even be able to comfort them, besides through my words. I was not allowed to touch them or hug them or anything. I had to keep my distance.

As I gathered my things in the hospital room, I noticed that Sammy had tears in his eyes. I think that my diagnosis was bringing back a lot of memories from a few years before when his mother was diagnosed with cancer. Cancer took his mother's life, and I'm sure my diagnosis hit a soft spot within him. I would later find out that Jackie said to him, "This is not like it was with your mother. They caught this problem early, and your wife is in the best possible place to conquer this." Jackie was not only guiding me in the medical protocol and educating doctors in the media protocol; she was also lifting the spirits of my husband

and comforting my family.

Jackie, Sammy, and Van all accompanied me as I boarded the elevator and went downstairs. When I walked into the conference room, my staff was standing around the perimeter of the room, and my fourteen players were sitting in chairs around a U-shaped formation of metal desks with wooden tops. I was met by confused looks from my players.

I told them that I was the patient they were seeing, and that I had been diagnosed with leukemia on Friday after practice. I found myself looking into the eyes of a lot of distraught faces. I spoke to them positively, hoping to give them some perspective and confidence in this little speed bump we were facing as a program.

"I will be out for a little while," I told them, "but Coach Calder will take over while I am in the hospital. You are in good hands. I will stay involved in the program and watch games and practice in whatever way I am allowed to, whether it's in person or from my hospital room on an iPad. I won't be far away."

Some girls were in a trance, shocked. Others were crying. I assured them that I would be okay and that they would be fine. "I'm gonna beat this thing and get back to coaching," I told them.

I felt that people in the room wanted to approach me and put their arms around me; unfortunately, they couldn't because of the germs.

"In the past, we've talked a lot about holding the rope for others," I said to them. "Will you hold the rope for me?"

The meeting was brief, lasting about fifteen minutes.

Seeing my team had made me even more eager to put this disease behind me. As I made my way back upstairs, I was ready to start fighting.

It was time to be hooked up to chemo. For an entire week. Nonstop.

- Chapter 5 -
ACCEPTANCE

"The metaphor for it metastasizes, too:
I am in the belly
of the beast, the belly of a whale, in some sterile
wilderness, desert
island, sand-blind; I am a thread in the deep
eye of a needle; in some
percussive otherworld that rises up
every time I exhale
and hold still my empty lungs."
~Claudia Emerson (1957–2014) from her book *Impossible Bottle*
(2015), UNC Greensboro MFA (1991)

Everything was changing. I don't think I realized it at the time; I was simply going from one thing to the next, doing what I *had* to do. Though my responsibilities had changed that weekend from basketball-related obligations to cancer-related obligations, what didn't change was the fact that I still had a lot of obligations. I was still running around.

That, of course, was about to change.

At the beginning of my treatments, the doctors and nurses at Lineberger had me switch rooms—to a corner room at the end of the hallway.

Room 4804.

The good people at Lineberger were helping me isolate myself a little bit more. We were still yet to tell the media of my diagnosis, and we asked the players and anyone else associated with the program not to post anything on social media until an official press release was published. Even in the hospital, I didn't want to be out and about in case someone might see me. Doctors said the new room would give me more privacy, away from the central flow of traffic in the wing. There was also a treadmill in a nook right outside my room; they knew I loved to exercise. Everything I needed was there.

As for my room, it had gigantic windows stretching from the ceiling to the floor all around the left wall. I could nearly see the football stadium, and I could see much of the UNC medical ward. The cancer center, by design, had windows in most of the patients' bedrooms and many of the lobbies—a reminder that light and life existed in the bleakest of circumstances. My bed was pinned up against the right wall, and a narrow couch ran across the back windows. The floor was a brownish orange.

This place, this corner room, would be my home for the next month.

At one point Dr. Pillsbury came over to visit me, and I remember him talking to Dr. Voorhees, pointing at him and saying, "If you need anything, let me know; you have to take care of her."

That evening, chemotherapy technicians—dressed like they were ready to handle nuclear waste—walked into my room carrying a long cylindrical tube full of a substance that looked like motor oil. They injected that viscous liquid into my port, and the first of my chemical treatments commenced.

Jackie explained it to me this way: "Sylvia, they are putting poison in your system, but it has to be poison in order to kill the cells that gave you leukemia."

I could feel the substance being flushed through my body. After a little bit of time, I felt like I had the flu or something.

That Sunday night, I fell asleep in my fourth-floor corner room, above a calm, dimly lit campus, while poison was being pumped into my body.

✺

I had trouble waking the next morning. I tried to open my eyes, but I couldn't. It was almost as if my eyelids were glued shut. They would sometimes blink open but only for a second before closing once more. I remember thinking to myself, *Wake up, wake up; this is just a bad*

dream.
　　But it wasn't a dream.
　　I had leukemia.
　　The fight had begun.

∽

Once I finally got my eyes open, I found myself lying in bed thinking about my dear friend, Kay Yow.

Kay, the legendary Hall of Fame North Carolina State coach who passed away in 2009 from Stage 4 breast cancer, always provided a model of grace and dignity under challenging circumstances.

I first met Kay in 1975 when she spoke at a women's basketball clinic at what was then Peace Junior College in Raleigh, North Carolina. At the time I heard her speak, I was in my first year coaching the women's basketball team at Francis Marion College in Florence, South Carolina. When I heard Kay tell the audience about her contract with PRO-Keds shoes, I remember being excited to learn that a women's basketball team could actually have a contract with a shoe company. Since my girls needed shoes as well, I spoke with Kay after her speech and explained that I was the coach at Francis Marion and that my girls were in desperate need of basketball shoes. I asked her if she could share with me the name of her contact at PRO-Keds. Kay was very gracious. She took my name, address, and the sizes of shoes that I needed.

One week after the clinic a huge box full of red and white PRO-Keds women's basketball shoes was delivered to my office. A note from Kay was inside: "Sylvia, my girls have more shoes than they can wear in a season, and since N.C. State and Francis Marion both wear the same shade of red, I thought you could use our surplus."

From that day forward Kay Yow was a great friend. Over the years, we stayed in touch and continued to build our relationship through the Women's Basketball Coaches Association and U.S.A. Basketball. When the head coaching position at UNC opened up, Kay recommended me. I was hired in 1986.

That same year, Kay asked me to be her assistant coach at the 1986 Goodwill Games and FIBA World Championships in Moscow. Two years later, in 1988, she asked me to be her assistant at the 1988 Olympic Games in Seoul, Korea. Of course, over the next two decades, our teams would go on to play against each other plenty of times in the ACC. What's interesting about that 1986 trip to Moscow, however, is that it might be the reason both of us got cancer. Let me explain…

Though I decided early on in my bout with leukemia that I would never ask God, "Why did I get cancer?", I did however find myself asking questions like, "*How* did I get cancer?" That first weekend, as I learned more and more about AML, I found it to be a curious question, one that continually stirred in the back of my mind.

There are typically four things that can cause leukemia: (1) genetics, (2) smoking, (3) pesticides, or (4) the environment. What's interesting is that leukemia does not run in my family, I have never smoked a single day in my life, and I haven't dealt with many pesticides. The only environmental thing I could think of was that Moscow, the site of the 1986 Goodwill Games, was close to Chernobyl, the site of the worst nuclear power plant accident in history, which had occurred less than two months prior to our time there. Sometimes it takes twenty years for environmental effects to be revealed in a person's health; for me it had been twenty-six.

Had we not gone to Moscow, would Kay Yow still be alive today?

Would I be here in this hospital room?

Though Kay died on January 24, 2009, her spirit has always been with me. And I suppose I could feel myself drawing strength from her dynamic optimism and joyful perspective as I lay in my hospital bed that morning.

∽

I guess you could say that Monday was a day of acceptance. When something bad or unexpected happens in our lives, we eventually must accept what has taken place, or we will never be able to live, or fight, in the present reality. Denial seems to be a natural reaction when experiencing the initial shock of things, but I knew that I could not fight cancer while denying that I had it. Though I am naturally a positive person—probably from coaching for so long and always trying to render up an element of hope for my team—I understand that others are not. Regardless, I think it's important to understand that constant denial, in any aspect of life, ultimately leads to victimization—and it is difficult to fight from the weak foundation of being a victim. It would make more sense to fight from a stronger foundation. To fully fight, I had to fully accept.

I find this to be true in coaching. Even as I write this, in the wake of the 2015–16 season, we have not only had to deal with players transferring because of the NCAA academic scandal; we have also had a lot of injuries to key players. As all this transpired, we had a choice: to adapt to the unexpected challenges or constantly dwell on what we no longer had. Uncontrolled circumstances forced us to adapt. We had a much better chance at excelling if we accepted the challenges and continued to fight alongside one another with the talent and chemistry we had. We adapted and pressed forward.

The people who seem to struggle most in this life are those who are resistant to change. Being resistant to change, however, is unrealistic. Things are always changing and will never stop changing. Even the seasons are changing. There is nothing in creation that isn't changing in some way.

∽

Although my world was spinning in chaos over the weekend, there were a few specific things that helped me accept my reality on Monday.

To begin, by now it was obvious from a medical standpoint that I was indeed a cancer patient. The doctors were implementing a strategy called "7 and 3" to combat my leukemia. This protocol was basically seven straight days of cytarabine treatments combined with three nights of daunorubicin, a high-powered chemo. Though this was a common strategy in other cancer treatments, it was fairly new with AML and had only been used in the medical field for about six months. Doctors frequently checked on me throughout the day—sometimes in fifteen-minute intervals—to make sure that I had not broken out with any rashes, as many patients do when they begin their chemo treatments. They checked my eyes because apparently chemo can have an adverse effect on them, and they also constantly evaluated my blood pressure, heart rate, and oxygen depth. They were afraid of reactions.

Monday was also the first day that I was not running around meeting with all sorts of people in preparation for my bout with cancer. I was restricted to the hospital, mostly my room. For a person like me, it was weird to be in *one* place for an entire day. Not only that, but I was restricted to the confines of the hospital for the second straight day. It was beginning to dawn on me: this place was my new "office" for planning, developing strategies, and refining my thinking—just like my office at Carmichael. This place was my new court for fighting and winning through how I fought.

Lastly, I think I began to accept my reality because UNC published a press release about my diagnosis on Monday afternoon. Here are the first few paragraphs:

> *University of North Carolina women's basketball head coach Sylvia Hatchell is temporarily stepping away from her on-the-court coaching responsibilities due to a recent diagnosis of leukemia.*

> *"I am going to be involved in a treatment plan established by Dr. Pete Voorhees, medical oncologist, and his team from the UNC Lineberger Comprehensive Cancer Center," says Hatchell. "I have the utmost confidence in my doctors. There is a reason why the North Carolina Cancer Hospital ranks as one of the top cancer facilities in the nation.*

> *"I will remain very much involved with my team and day-to-day operations here at UNC and expect to return to my sideline responsibilities as soon as possible. My veteran staff and team will be well prepared and meet any challenges until my return. Don't forget I am a Tar Heel woman!"*

It was necessary to get the word out as soon as possible so that people had clarity. When news of my leukemia was made public, my cell phone never stopped ringing. I received calls, messages, texts, and emails from a host of people wishing me well. Anne Graham Lotz told me that she had people from all over the world praying for me.

I could feel the prayers strengthening me. I could feel the prayers bringing me a sense of peace.

I think that everyone else's knowledge helped me comprehend my reality. It was no longer my secret, my fight.

It was *our* fight now.

- Chapter 6 -
THINKING SOUNDLY IN THE UNKNOWN

"For God has not given us the spirit of fear; but of power, and of love, and of a sound mind."
2 Timothy 1:7 (KJV)

"Most of the time we think we're sick, it's all in the mind."
~Thomas Wolfe (1900–1938), UNC Class of 1920, novelist

As I accepted my new reality and began to mentally prepare for my fight with leukemia, I was reminded of a story that one of my neighbors told me the year before...

Our UNC team was approaching the end of the 2011–12 season, and we were ranked one of the top five in the country. We were set to face Maryland on the road in a double-header on Friday night and Duke at home on Sunday afternoon—two tough games in three days. We unfortunately got smoked by Maryland on Friday, didn't get back to Chapel Hill until the wee hours of the morning on Saturday, and then spun around and had practice at ten o'clock in the morning to prepare for our matchup against Duke on Sunday. In the midst of all this scrambling around and sifting through my inner anguish from losing to Maryland, I had completely forgotten that my neighbors were hosting a birthday party for me on Saturday afternoon at one o'clock. Sure, it wasn't the best timing for a birthday party. Celebrating my birthday was the last thing on my mind, but not all of them understood the basketball world, so it was a kind gesture nonetheless.

After no sleep, we did our film work at ten o'clock in the morning on Saturday and then had practice. At one o'clock I was standing on the court coaching my team when my cell phone started to buzz in my pocket. I looked at it, saw a number of missed calls and text messages, and remembered that my neighbors were hosting a birthday party for me. We were nearing the end of practice anyway, so I finished up leading the women through the remainder of their drills, ran home, changed clothes, and went to my neighbor's house.

There were probably fifty or sixty people there. I walked in and started shaking people's hands and talking to those in attendance, apologizing for being late. I made my way through the house toward the kitchen, where I knew that my neighbors, an elderly couple named Eddie and Patsy, would most likely be. Eddie was probably eighty-five or ninety at the time; Patsy was in her eighties. They were indeed there in the kitchen, so I sat down next to them at a round, wooden table. They wished me happy birthday, and I thanked them.

I sat with them for a while, and at one point we began talking about Black Mountain, one of my favorite places in the world to visit. I told them about my cabin there and the blueberry patch that helped raise money for Lineberger.

"Coach," Eddie eventually said, "I don't have a birthday present for you, so what I'm going to give you is a little advice."

Great, I thought to myself, *another person is going to try to tell me how to coach my team since we lost last night to Maryland on national television.*

"You talk about Black Mountain and all that stuff," Eddie began, "and that reminds me of when my bride of sixty years and I got married and went up to the mountains for our honeymoon."

Eddie reached over and touched Patsy on the arm. She smiled.

"I remember driving back through Black Mountain," he continued, "and my new bride wanted some ice cream. So I stopped at a little soda place in Black Mountain."

"Eddie," I said, "I know exactly what you are talking about. Right there on Cherry Street. Now it's an eye vision place."

"That's right," he said, "so I went inside to get some ice cream. I bought two cones of ice cream, paid, and began walking out. That's when the door came flying open and three little kids came running in. They each picked out the type of ice cream that they wanted, and I noticed that one little boy didn't have enough money. Tears started streaming down his face, and he dropped his head in embarrassment and disappointment.

"When I got back to the car, I told Patsy what I had witnessed in the ice cream store. I said to her, 'You know what? I should have bought that little boy some ice cream…I'll be right back.' So I walked back in to find him. But he wasn't there. I asked the lady behind the counter, 'Did that boy that was in here end up finding some money for his ice cream?' She said, 'No, he didn't.' I said, 'Do you know who he was?' She said, 'No, I don't.' I said, 'Do you know where they went?' She said, 'No, they went outside, probably up the street or something.'

"I went up and down Cherry Street looking for the boy. I walked into every shop and every store, talking to every person that I saw, hoping to find the boy. I wanted to buy him some ice cream."

Eddie had tears in his eyes, and he lowered his head.

After a period of silence, Patsy put her hand on Eddie's back, looked at me intently, and said, "Coach, he's still looking for that little boy today."

"Coach," Eddie continued, "my birthday present is some advice: take advantage of the opportunities that God puts in front of you every day, because once they're gone, they're gone."

"Eddie," I said, "that's the best birthday present I've ever received."

∽

Eddie's story has always stuck with me.

Opportunities hardly ever look the way we expect them to look—and life hardly ever looks the way we expect it to look; therefore, there are opportunities all throughout life. As Scottish geologist and writer Hugh Miller once said, "Problems are only opportunities with thorns on them."

To be honest, it was sometimes difficult to remain positive during those first few days in the hospital because there was so much that was up in the air regarding the direction the doctors would take in treating my cancer. The most pressing matter for the doctors was finding a way to get me into remission as quickly as possible, but they had no idea how. They were still awaiting the results from my FLT3 test, which in layman's terms was an in-depth breakdown of my genetics, blood, and bone marrow, which would give the doctors some direction in their strategy for me. Would I need a bone marrow transplant? Would I need additional consolidation treatments? Was there another strategy they would have to implement?

Another vital aspect of the FLT3 test was that, once my results came in, doctors would have a better idea of my chance of survival. Upon my initial diagnosis, my chance of survival was about thirty percent. I did not personally look up statistics or ask the doctors to reveal them to me, but I had heard the statistics in passing and had seen them in newspaper articles about me. Though I was trying to remain positive, this was still extremely daunting. It usually takes ten days to two weeks for a patient's FLT3 results to be finalized. I hadn't even been in the hospital for three days, and it already felt like an eternity. I was undoubtedly in the thick of the unknown.

In the meantime, my doctors were frantically trying to find me a bone marrow match, just in case the FLT3 results came back positive. First, doctors contacted my two brothers and my sister to be tested. Typically, each sibling has a twenty-five percent chance of being a perfect match for another sibling. Having three siblings, one might conclude that I had a favorable, seventy-five percent chance of finding a match within my family. Unfortunately, there was no suitable match.

Next, they began trying to find me a bone marrow match through Be The Match, the national donor registry to help fight leukemia. A week went by. Still nothing.

No bone marrow match.

No FLT3 results.

Since my diagnosis, I was yet to receive any good news. Only bad news. What would become of me?

Around this time, I remember a doctor named Ben Vincent, who was part of the team of doctors that was assembled by Dr. Voorhees, visiting me in my hospital room and noticing a Bible beside my bed.

"Are you a Christian?" he asked me.

"Yes, I am," I said.

"Can I pray with you?" he asked me.

"I would love that," I said.

Dr. Vincent put his hand on my shoulder, and as Sammy and my friend Mary Lou gathered around me, he prayed the sweetest, most sincere prayer, asking God to lead the doctors in the right direction. I felt a transcending peace in that moment. It was a reminder to me that

I was in God's hands. After he finished the prayer and left the room, I looked at Sammy, teary-eyed, and said, "This place is amazing."

∽

Around this time, I remember listening to a sermon by pastor and evangelist David Jeremiah, whose sister Mary Alice had been a successful women's basketball coach, and writing this thought down on a piece of paper to keep next to my bed: "A godly woman in the center of God's will is immortal until God is through with her."

Though being cooped up in a hospital went entirely against the to-and-fro, planned-to-the-minute, hustle-and-bustle lifestyle I was used to, I had to force myself to believe that I was in the exact place that I needed to be, that God intended me to be.

When we are uncomfortable, it is easy for fear to fester. And there are two types of fear: one that drives us and one that stops us. I believed that nothing in my life was an accident; therefore, fear couldn't stop me.

As uncomfortable as I might have felt being trapped in the hospital and living in the thick of the unknown, I had to believe Dr. Jeremiah's quote—that I was right where I needed to be. I had to believe Eddie—that opportunities to help others would come from this. Though I was no longer on the sideline coaching my team in the game of basketball—something that had been my purpose in life for decades—I conditioned myself to believe that God would use the "thorn in my side" to open up other opportunities that could help or coach others. As badly as I wanted to put my disease behind me, as desperately as I wanted clarity from the FLT3 test, my leukemia was another chapter in my story—quite possibly the most important one.

∽

During that first week of chemo treatment, I was in a little bit of pain. I experienced some nausea and fatigue and contracted a severe case of mucositis. I was told that the most difficult part would be when chemo did its work in the coming days. They called this a "dive"—when the chemotherapy knocks down your immune system, attempts to flush out the cancer cells, and in doing so eradicates your white blood cells and neutrophils to the point that you don't have the strength to fight a single germ. This was usually the most trying time for cancer patients. Often, it isn't the cancer that kills a patient but rather the patient's inability to handle the chemotherapy treatments and fight infections.

I could not dread the future; nor could I allow my mind to dwell on the present uncertainty. I had to focus on the little things and prepare mentally for the coming storm. I've heard it said, "Life isn't about surviving the storm but learning to dance in the rain." Though I could not control how my body would react to the treatments, I could control my mentality. Though I could not control the results of the FLT3 test, I could control whether or not I allowed the unknown to absorb my joy, as it often does with people.

In fact, I understood that my mentality might even affect how my body handled the intensity of the treatments. Everything was connected. It was all intertwined. There was no need for me to let the unknown cause anxiety within me; no amount of worrying would help me get out of the unknown any quicker. Worry never added a day to anyone's life. In her book, *Clippings from My Notebook*, Corrie ten Boom wrote: "Worry does not empty tomorrow of its sorrow. It empties today of its strength."

As scared as I might have been, I also knew that I was in good hands. If there is one word that describes the people at Lineberger, it might be this: dedicated. They are always conducting groundbreaking research and seem to be on the front lines of pioneering and innovation. (In 2014, Lineberger was the seventh largest recipient nationally of National Institutes of Health funding on the study and treatment of cancer in children and adults; and in 2015, *U.S. News & World Report* ranked the cancer center thirty-second in the nation out of 5,000 hospitals.)

Though it was uncharted waters for me to be entirely reliant on the care of others, I believed that I was in the best of care and that I was in the right place. In the chaos and uncertainty, I tried to remind myself of the positives.

∽

After my first round of treatments, I knew that it was only a matter of time before my hair began to fall out. One day, a doctor named Ned Sharpless, the director of the UNC Lineberger Comprehensive Cancer

Center, was checking on me, and I asked him, "Ned, when will my hair start to fall out?"

"When did they start chemo?" he asked.

"October 13," I told him.

"Probably on next Sunday afternoon at about three o'clock," he said.

Wow, that's precise, I thought to myself.

Sure enough, at three o'clock on the last Sunday in October, I reached up on top of my head and pulled out a handful of hair.

These guys are good, I remember thinking.

By Monday morning, I had hair all over my pillow.

I recognize that this can sometimes be a sobering thing for cancer patients, as normalcy fades and reality settles in. The sudden loss of hair seems to visibly demonstrate a complete loss of control. Such a seemingly mindless thing I had always taken for granted—hair—suddenly became a poignant reminder of a disease that was attempting to kill me.

That morning, however, I realized that this was one of those unexpected opportunities I mentioned earlier, where I could choose positivity instead of dwelling on something that I couldn't control. There are many mental crossroads like this each day—especially when you are dealing with a looming struggle—that will dictate your thinking patterns and your state of well-being. That being said, I decided to throw a party.

I called my longtime hair stylist, Wanda Guthrie, on Monday morning and asked her, "Can you come over here and bring your shears? We're going to have a head-shaving party!"

Wanda came over, and I invited doctors and nurses to join me for a "Shave Coach Hatchell's Head Party." A big, white sheet was spread out on the floor, and I sat on a chair on top of the sheet as Wanda shaved my head.

She shaved one side, and I thought, "Man, who turned the air conditioner on?" I had always heard that you lose a lot of your body heat through your head. Well, when they shaved one side of my head, I felt the coolness immediately.

Next, Wanda took the hair left on the other side of my head and flipped it over onto the shaved side. I looked like a punk rocker.

Then she shaved most of the other side, leaving hair on top, which gave me a Mohawk. I looked like Mr. T, the actor and professional wrestler from the eighties.

Next, she shaved the Mohawk until I had a rat's tail in the back. I'm not sure what I looked like.

When Wanda shaved off the rat's tail, she painted "Go Heels" on the back of my head. It was fitting that she did so because we had an exhibition game against Carson-Newman on Wednesday. Now I looked like Kojak, a completely bald television character from the seventies.

Overall, the party was a lot of fun. Parties are always fun. Even parties in the hospital.

∽

I believe that you can change the world by changing your attitude. I would echo what Christian pastor and author Chuck Swindoll once said: "The only thing we can do is play on the one string we have, and that is our attitude...I am convinced that life is ten percent what happens to me and ninety percent how I react to it. And so it is with you... we are in charge of our attitudes."

Your attitude is the one thing that you can control.

But it's a choice. A decision.

A week after the start of my treatments, I could feel my body beginning to take the "dive" that people warned me about. My numbers were dropping. Simply getting out of bed began to require more and more willpower. We still had not received my FLT3 results.

How weak would I become? How bad would this be? How poorly would I feel? What would the FLT3 reveal?

Strength was becoming something that no longer came naturally. It was something that I had to discover deep within. You find how much of a winner you are at heart when you are infected by something like cancer, when your own body feels defeated. I was determined to maintain a winning mentality through it all. What do you have to lose by adopting a good attitude in life? Things in this life will inevitably go wrong. Wouldn't it make sense to brew up positivity and perspective in our minds so that we can better handle life's trials and maintain some sense of hope in the midst of them? Businesswoman Mary Kay Ash once said: "Don't limit yourself. Many people limit themselves to what they think they can do. You can go as far as your mind lets you. What you believe, remember, you can achieve."

I was determined to be a winner.

And winning always starts in the mind.

I always recruited winners. Not only would I try to recruit great players, but I would also try to recruit great players who were on great teams. These types of players not only knew how to win but *expected* to win. Winning is an unquenchable thirst, but losing is a disease. That is true in sports and is also true of just about everything in this life.

There are two types of people: positive people and negative people. There are two types of thinkers: winners and losers. Some people, unfortunately, just aren't happy unless they're unhappy. Their comfort zone is being miserable. These types of people always seem to be complaining with a "woe is me" attitude. I don't like hearing it, honestly. I don't like being around people like that.

I actually have a loud plastic clicker that I sometimes keep in my pocket, and if I hear players on my team talking negatively amongst one another or complaining to our coaches, I begin to annoyingly click the clicker. I obviously believe there is profound value in raw emotion, expressing yourself, and moving through the process of grief, as heavy as that can be, but if someone is complaining just to complain, whether it's gossip or victimization or whatever, I would rather not hear it. So I click.

There's an old song called "Keep On the Sunny Side" that my mother always sang to me when I was a child. It was written by Ada Blenkhorn in 1899, and the chorus goes like this:

Keep on the sunny side, always on the sunny side
Keep on the sunny side of life
It will help us every day, it will brighten all the way
If we keep on the sunny side of life

Positivity has always been a cornerstone in my life. I wasn't going to allow the natural challenges that come with existence in this fallen world to remove that cornerstone. My body might have been taking a dive, my immune system might have been crashing, but nothing could stop me from discovering what I was made of in my heart and in my mind. I was determined to keep on the sunny side, no matter how bad things became. No matter what my future entailed.

- Chapter 7 -
COMMIT TO A GAME PLAN

"I encourage my players to treat games away from home as a wonderful challenge. I like to tell my team, 'Let's go into their living room and steal their brownies.' It's all about having the confidence and attitude that I can beat your butt anytime, anywhere, anyplace, anyhow.... The bottom line is that I want my players to understand that at some point in every game, somebody's going to give in, and I don't ever want it to be us. We want to be the last team standing."
~Roy Williams, UNC Class of 1972, UNC men's basketball coach
(2003–current)

One day I was resting in bed when Dr. Voorhees walked into my hospital room. Sammy was sitting on the corner of my bed. Van was sitting on the couch.

I noticed that Dr. Voorhees was sporting a wide grin on his face, and he proceeded to tell us that my FLT3 results were overwhelmingly positive. Based on what they had found, he believed that my survival rate had risen from around thirty to sixty percent, and because of my good genetics, he believed I had gone up to seventy percent.

Van had a big smile, and he pumped his fist. Sammy and I were crying joyful tears. In a single moment, we learned that my survival rate had more than doubled—the first good news since my diagnosis. Because Dr. Voorhees was always honest and blunt with me, I knew that I could trust the news that he delivered. He always gave me the truth—from the seriousness that he stressed to me upon my initial diagnosis to the joy that exuded from him upon the revelation of my FLT3 results.

He was someone I could trust, the best type of doctor to have.

After being blindsided by the diagnosis and haunted by the unknown during my first week or so in the hospital, the positive news was a glimmer of hope in a sea of confusion and heaviness. What a joyful moment. I knew that the road ahead would still be long and painful, but the FLT3 results seemed to reinforce the positivity that I was trying to implement into my thinking.

Doctors were still looking to find me a bone marrow match but weren't having any luck. Though this was Plan A, my FLT3 results led them to believe that they might be able to pursue Plan B and still eradicate my body of its cancer. What Plan B entailed, they said, was a series of consolidation treatments following my initial 7 and 3 treatment in the hospital. This meant more chemo, and it was undoubtedly the longer road (and perhaps more painful), but it was encouraging to know that because of my FLT3 results, Plan B could still work. I felt fortunate that there were other options.

I was told that if a bone marrow match was not found, I would most likely have to undergo at least four consolidation treatments. Through it all, the doctors' primary goal was to get me into remission.

∽

In the coming days, though my body was beginning to feel weaker than it ever had before as my immune system took a dive, the FLT3 results gave me new life in my spirit. Yes, the realization that the consolidation treatments (Plan B) might keep me off the court for a longer amount of time was difficult to hear, but I was thankful for the clarity and for the encouraging news about my survival rate. I was indeed used to experiencing meaning and purpose through coaching—which had been my life's work—but I knew I had to reconstruct that paradigm in the hospital.

One day when Dr. Voorhees was talking to me about the process of my cancer treatments—how I was in the middle of my initial dive from the first round of chemo and would have at least four more consolidation treatments—I said to him, "It sounds a lot like the basketball season. You have your preseason practices, exhibition games, the non-conference season, the regular season, the conference season, the conference tournament, and finally the NCAA tournament. You can't focus on the season without good practices in the preseason; you can't have a good postseason without focusing on the season."

He told me that my metaphor was a good one.

So I decided to commit myself to a new game plan.

I am not a perfectionist. I am not an idealist. But I must be able to commit myself to a game plan. If I can do this, if I can find a focus point, I can more easily remain in the present.

My primary game plan was no longer coaching; it was beating cancer. This simple truth, as basic as it might seem, helped me not to feel as if I was missing out on my truest calling in life: coaching.

When we endure a setback in life, it is natural to experience feelings of worthlessness or purposelessness. But I was right where I needed to be. God was directing my life. As Dr. David Jeremiah's quote said, I was in the center of His will, though little sense as that made to me at the time. Of course, nothing that is of God should make perfect sense. His thoughts are not our thoughts; His ways are not our ways (Isaiah 55:8–9).

I wasn't trying to get back to my normal life. This was now my new normal. And that was okay. Exhausting myself with thoughts about getting back to how my life was would only cause anxiety and discontentment to well up within me; dedicating myself to giving my all in this new normal would help me thrive in the present. Why waste energy over something that I could not control? To fight, I had to first commit to a mental game plan, one that I would be dedicated to executing each and every day. Mentally, I committed to Plan B and tried to position myself in a way that would best help execute that plan.

It seems that much of the anxiety and restlessness that many people feel in life comes from the inability to adopt a new game plan in life's unexpected circumstances. Our situation in life will never be perfect. But somehow we must find a way to experience meaning and fulfillment in the present. For me, that meant focusing on doing everything I possibly could—mentally and physically—to defeat cancer.

Yes, I had built my life on encouraging young women through the art of coaching. Coaching basketball was my normal. But instead of allowing myself to be negatively affected by what I no longer had—something I couldn't control—I had to commit to something elsewhere. Battling cancer was my new normal. In this life all that we can ask of ourselves is to do the best we can in each situation that is presented to us. The rest is beyond our control. Of course, sometimes it's vital for one to change his or her situation, but most of the time—like my cancer diagnosis—there was nothing that could be done but commit myself to a new purpose.

It is easy to become distracted by how we feel that life should be. But the result is that we spend our lives exhausting ourselves attempting to attain a far-off reality. The truth is that life is hardly ever how we pictured it. The truth is that reality is now.

In the hospital, I was challenged to find meaning and joy in the midst of life's imperfections. I've heard it said that champions in life are not crowned by who can throw the biggest punch; rather, champions are crowned by who can take the biggest punch, get back up, and keep fighting. Endurance wins, not strength. Steadiness prevails, not flashiness.

For me, the word "champion" was always associated with coaching. But my new game plan involved becoming a champion in how I fought cancer. Taking the punches. Fighting through the doubts and anxieties. Pressing on despite the physical weakness I felt. And getting back up again and again and again.

What I didn't know was that the fight was only beginning.

- Chapter 8 -
KEEP MOVING

Fight!
We Fight for Alma Mater
Fight!
'Til Day Is Through
We Sing the Praises Carolina
Fight! Fight! for NCU
~University of North Carolina fight song

My system bottomed out.

Never had I felt so fatigued, so weak. It was strange to go from being in the best shape of my life to suddenly not even wanting to get out of bed. I even lost some of my memory. They call it chemo brain. There were times when someone would walk into my hospital room and I wouldn't even know who she was—even though she was a good friend of mine! I had to tear through the cobwebs in my mind before I arrived at a conclusion.

Everyone reacts differently to chemo. Some break out in rashes. Some get sores in their mouths. The worst side effect for me was chemotherapy's toll on my throat. My throat went completely raw. It hurt to even swallow. It felt like the insides of my esophagus had been severely burnt. I eventually started drinking a sort of numbing medication that they called "magic mouthwash" just so I could eat and drink and stay nourished.

Every morning, doctors would come into my room and run blood tests—writing my numbers (for neutrophils, platelets, and white blood cells) down on a board. As weak as I felt some days, I made a commitment in my mind to keep moving, to get out of my bed every day and exercise. I was determined not to be a stereotypical patient who was bound to a hospital bed. I wouldn't even wear a hospital gown or pajamas because I didn't want to be affiliated with the idea of weakness. I wore gym shorts, T-shirts, or warm-ups. I didn't want to do anything that made me feel as if I was a victim. I wasn't. Life is imperfect. I had my game plan, and I was fully committed to doing everything I could to execute it.

During this time, I would often walk down the fourth-floor hallway, past the forty rooms or so, in the cancer wing. As I peered into different patients' rooms, I was sometimes shocked at the sights that I saw. Often times, the patients would seem to be eternally bed-ridden, as if paralyzed by their situation, with their blinds closed and their lights off. Their curtains would sometimes be drawn around their beds. Total darkness. Isolation. Hopelessness. Some of the environments I witnessed were so dark and depressing. The thought would sometimes cross my mind: *How are these people ever going to get well if they don't get out of their beds?*

It was all cyclical: the gloomy environment affected their mentalities, their hopeless mentalities made them unwilling to get out of bed, and their stagnancy made their environment even gloomier, even more foreboding. I understand that some patients, sadly, were far weaker than I was and didn't have a choice but to stay in bed. Yet many of them *did* have a choice but chose to sulk in their situation. I've heard it said that if you change your habits, you can change your limits. In this unfamiliar situation, it was up to me to change my habits.

There were some days where it felt like a Mack Truck had run over me—the last thing I felt like doing was getting out of bed—but in my mind I was determined never to succumb to darkness or inactivity. My bed was only good for one thing: sleeping. I would nap in my bed and sleep there at night—that's it. If I was too weak to be on my feet but didn't want to sleep, I would sit in a nearby chair. I made a commitment to myself that I would keep moving. I knew that my ability to keep moving, regardless of how I felt, would influence my thinking and help me to never feel helpless or like a victim to my disease.

Exercising was my demonstration to the cancer that it did not have the upper hand. The disease might have forced me to enter chemotherapy, which in turn made me *feel* frail and weak, but my feelings did not have to dictate what I did or didn't do. What mattered most was my spirit.

And at the core of my spirit was God, and therefore I had access to power and strength and positivity and peace. My ability or inability to live out of my spirit, not my feelings, would determine whether or not I made it out of my bed and approached each day with a mindset that was marked by courage and boldness.

∽

One person who pushed me in this area was a man named Dr. Claudio Battaglini, an associate professor of exercise and sport science at UNC. Claudio was a kind, Brazilian professor who directed the Integrative Exercise Oncology Laboratory. He had a high voice and a great head of thick, black hair. He was a bundle of energy. He had coached Olympic champions and other professionals in their respective sports for almost two decades, but in the pursuit of his coaching career, he discovered a passion for helping cancer patients and applying exercise science to oncology.

In his and his team's research over the years, they discovered, through science and statistical analysis, that regular exercise among breast cancer patients led to an increased survival rate. Claudio and his team also found that exercise could influence some of the physiological systems in patients throughout treatment and could even alleviate symptoms and reduce recurrence.

Because of all of this, he helped develop the "Get REAL (Recreation Exercise Active Living) & HEEL" program, an initiative dedicated to exercise and educational therapy for cancer patients at UNC Lineberger. The program was originally created for breast cancer patients, but it had grown to include patients with prostate cancer, colorectal cancer, and blood disorders.

Before my diagnosis with leukemia, I had followed a strict exercise routine, meeting with a personal trainer twice a week. Since I was prone to let my busy schedule interfere with my own workouts, I told the trainer that I would pay him double if I missed one of our appointments. Needless to say, I did not miss many workouts. When I began my chemotherapy, I did not want to stop working out just because the poison might make my body weak.

Cancer changed how I was involved in coaching but not my ability to still be involved, and I also believed that though cancer changed *how* I exercised, it did not need to stop me from exercising. Given the success of Get REAL & HEEL, I asked Claudio to develop an exercise program for me. The original program was designed to provide exercise for patients after chemotherapy treatments, but the plan he developed for me included workouts while I was in the hospital receiving chemotherapy.

Claudio would come to the hospital almost every day. I would warm up for ten minutes or so, and then he and I would work with resistance bands or free weights for strength training. Then we would always go out in the hallway and walk around.

Seventeen laps around the fourth-floor cancer wing. One mile.

I always wore my mask, and I remained hooked up to an IV stand that I lovingly named "Stanley"—my shag dance partner. When Claudio and I went for a walk, we took turns pushing "Stanley." Sometimes I felt so weak that I would use both Claudio and Stanley as my crutches. Every day that I worked out, I felt better.

Don't get me wrong: many days when I woke up, I felt that there was no possible way that I could make it one lap around that cancer wing, let alone seventeen. But with Claudio's help, and I suppose my own stubbornness, I always got out of bed. Claudio was motivational and encouraging each time he led me through a workout. He would say to me, "You're gonna get better; you got this; we're gonna get you better."

And I almost always made it seventeen laps, as daunting as it sometimes felt.

Step by step.

One after another.

Exercise was invaluable for me. It fueled my mind with truths about myself. No matter how I felt, exercising helped me to believe that I wasn't helpless or hopeless or worthless. I was strong. I could still accomplish something, even in my weakness. Especially on those really difficult days when I didn't think that I had it in me, exercising reminded me that, as cliché as it might sound, I could do anything I put my mind to. As long as I was exercising and getting out of bed, my mind reigned over my body.

One day Claudio entered my room and I told him, "Claudio, I don't know if I can get out of bed today. I'm so weak."

"I understand," he said to me comfortingly. "But let's just get out of bed for a little bit. You can hold my arm and we'll walk around the hall."

As I slowly rose to my feet, using every ounce of energy that I had, I told him, "I don't know if I can do this."

"We'll go slow," he consoled. "We'll walk a little, talk for a bit, and then you can come back to your bed."

I grabbed his arm, we exited my room into the hallway with my mask on, and we began to walk. Slowly but intentionally. One step at a time.

One lap.

Two laps.

Three.

Four.

Five.

Before I knew it, we had walked nine or ten laps.

When we returned to my room, I was completely exhausted. Out of breath. No energy remaining. I couldn't believe that walking a half-mile around an air-conditioned hallway felt as if I had run a marathon. What was happening to me?

"Sit down in that chair over there, and we'll do a little bit of stretching," Claudio gently said.

After stretching, I mustered up whatever sliver of strength that I had left and did some exercises with my resistance bands. Again, before I knew it, I had been exercising for fifteen minutes.

By the time I was finished, I felt better, but I was wiped. I slept for several hours in a nearby chair. However, it was a lesson that strength is not found in a feeling but rather in your willpower, your heart, and your spirit.

∽

Things will happen in each of our lives that push us to the very edge of our willpower and internal strength. When these times arise, it seems that we arrive at a crossroads—often for several days or months or years at a time—as to whether we will keep moving or cave to our feeling of weakness and, in doing so, accept defeat. Sometimes we need others to push us. Healing, whether it be physical or emotional, is not always a process that we can control, but we can control whether or not we keep moving. It is a conscious decision. Fighting is a choice.

The great challenge in life's hardships is not to bypass the struggle but rather to move *through* it. What I find most interesting about the often-quoted Psalm 23 is that it acknowledges that the difficult times in our lives are not things that we are supposed to ignore or avoid: "Even though I walk *through* the valley of the shadow of death..."

To move through something, it takes a series of steps, one after another, no matter how small they might be. Just like walking around that hallway. Often times, it is all that we can do to consciously decide, each and every day, to move. It does not matter whether we feel as if we are crawling or sprinting. All that matters is that we keep moving: through the pain, even if it becomes worse, and through the storm, even if it is into the eye.

Whatever resistance you are experiencing today, don't avoid it; move *through* it. Metaphorically lying in bed is a way of avoiding it, of allowing the pain to paralyze your willpower. Moving through whatever you're facing might take a long time. I had no idea how long I would be fighting leukemia, how long I would be removed from coaching, how long I would feel weak.

But I could keep moving.

You can too.

- Chapter 9 -
PRESENCE, PATIENCE, AND PERSEVERANCE

"I think the real free person in society is one that's disciplined. It's the one that can choose; that is the free one."
-Dean Smith (1931–2015), UNC men's basketball coach (1961–1977)

Though the chemo was taking a serious toll on my body, what was most difficult for me during this time was the sudden change in my lifestyle.

When I first started my treatments, I remember one of the doctors telling me, "What's going to be most difficult for you is getting through cabin fever."

He was exactly right.

To be honest, some days—many days—it felt like I was trapped in those hospital walls. Cabin fever was a real thing. It was already late October. The season had already begun. I hadn't missed a game since 1989, when I gave birth to my and Sammy's only son, Van. And now I was resting much of the day in a fifteen-by-twenty-foot room.

I missed seeing my girls on the team and my staff on a daily basis. I missed having heart-to-heart talks with my players in my office about what they were going through. I missed the daily challenges and the daily routine. I missed working toward a goal, the ultimate goal, as a unit on the hardwood. I missed the feeling of trying to solve a puzzle and the exhilarating feeling of solving it. I missed the chase. More than anything, I missed the relationships.

Yes, I was staying involved in the program. I watched practice on my tablet each day and met with my staff via video conference; I also made calls to my staff and to my girls, and all of this was good for me, but it wasn't the same. Though Lineberger was not even a half-mile away from Carmichael Arena, I felt like I was on the other side of the country. I missed coaching. I missed my life as I had known it.

I also missed the simple things in life I had taken for granted, like being with my longtime golden retriever, Maddie. One of my neighbors, Joy Farley, who, interestingly, was an actress on a couple soap operas, was a godsend during this time and would often take care of Maddie since Sammy was sometimes out of town with his coaching duties. Almost every day, she would check on Maddie at the house and send me a video or picture with the text "Your Daily Dose of Maddie." Maddie is the daughter I never had. I felt very low after my rounds of chemotherapy, and Joy's "Maddie texts" helped keep my spirits up.

Through it all, I continued to believe that God was sovereign, that He did not make mistakes, that there was a reason for all of this. A long time ago, I told God that I was all His to use the way He wanted to use me. Yes, the winds were swirling and the rain was coming down, but God was there with me. In the eye of the storm, I was also in the center of His will. In Janice Mock's book *Not All Bad Comes to Harm You*, there's a quote from a man named Daniel Achinsky: "Only in the storm can you see the art of the real sailor."

I don't know of a higher calling than for God to pick you and use you to reach out to other people, to use your brokenness to help others. I had no idea how God might use my trial to help others at the time, but I knew I had to remain faithful to His plan. The most important hour was the present.

∽

Never in my life had I experienced something comparable to the cabin fever I experienced in the hospital. Cabin fever, in a clinical sense, has its root in anxiety—the fear that spawns from the overwhelming feeling of having no escape. Essentially cabin fever is birthed in the discontent we feel in a current situation.

I had no idea when my situation might change. Sometimes it felt as if there was no escape. I was used to moving one hundred miles per hour from one thing to the next, but now I had no control of when I might be back on the sidelines. I was at the mercy of the cancer. I had to do whatever the cancer required me to do. And for now, that meant being inside a hospital for at least four weeks straight—going nowhere.

Tens of thousands of thoughts enter our minds each day—and this can be heightened when we experience something negative or traumatic—but I had the choice as to whether or not to cling to some of these thoughts and allow them to carry me into the thick of anxiety or the pit of despair.

I tried to dissect each negative thought that entered my mind and turn it into something positive. Yes, I was stuck in a hospital, but I knew that God had a plan and that it was an honor to be a part of His plan. I had no idea what was ahead on this unfamiliar road, but I knew that God could take the most overwhelming situation and use it for good (Romans 8:28); this, in fact, is when God does His best work.

Yes, I was weak, but in my weakness, I was strong in Him (2 Corinthians 12:10). I dedicated myself to the discipline of never dreading what I didn't have and never allowing myself to give into the thinking that I was missing out in life because of my situation.

When something unexpected happens in life, it is easy to obsess over the future—you know, when things are better, when the struggle is over, when the terror is in the rearview window. But I found it urgent to remain in the present.

I remember thinking about my basketball team and the things I had taught them. Even in the current 2013–14 season, when we were rated No. 12 in the *Associated Press* preseason rankings, I knew that it would be communicated to the girls that it was necessary to take the season game by game. One step at a time. Never focusing on anything more than the current film session or the current practice or the current game. Success is often dependent on a person's (or team's) ability to remain in the present. To focus on the here and now.

Especially when it pertains to illness, it's tempting to think about the future—the "ifs" and "whens" of when life will return to normal. But there was no sense in my doing so. This was my life now. And it didn't matter whether I approved of it or not. My mental and emotional stability, which would inevitably affect my physical health, would be determined by my ability or inability to remain in the present. Though I looked forward in anticipation to the opportunities that God might open up as part of His plan, it was vital, for my health, and sanity, that

I remained in the present.

Presence plus patience plus perseverance equals a good game plan for just about anything in life.

∽

My grandfather was a carpenter and a builder. I love to build too. I drew up the plans for my and Sammy's house in Chapel Hill, and when I visit the beach, I often sit on the shoreline reading books about house planning and architecture. When I was a child, I used to sit in church and draw house plans. Today, I have a whole stack of books about house plans and all kinds of things like that. I love it.

Obviously, this is one reason why I like coaching as well. From the very start, the exhilaration of building something is what drew me to the profession. At Francis Marion, I did whatever it took to be successful. With no assistant coaches, I wore out four of my own cars simply from recruiting. I drove the bus, swept the floor, washed the uniforms. You do whatever it takes to be successful, to build something that you can be proud of. If I'm not building something, I struggle to experience meaning. I am always looking ahead. I am a visionary. I love trying to move toward the next level of success.

That feeling of building something obviously came to a halt during that first month in the hospital. I was still involved in the program, but I wasn't as hands-on as I was used to. For the first time, I had little control *of* my life and could hardly plan ahead *in* my life. I had to stick to the game plan that I had already committed to—one that had gone from building a basketball program to simply surviving.

This struggle required a lot of patience. Like any trial, merely getting through it is a marathon, not a sprint. By now I understood that my disease was serious and life-threatening. Patience is not merely waiting for things to get better; patience often requires enduring the hard times with the hope that there is a light at the end of the tunnel. I had to commit to one thing at a time in my new normal, no matter how small or petty or meaningless it seemed in light of what I was used to completing and accomplishing in my former normal.

∽

Big things happen when you do the little things.

That's what I've always told my teams.

We couldn't control whether or not a call went our way, or whether or not one of our star players got injured, or whether a last-second shot fell through the nylon or rimmed out, but we could control the little things. We could control whether or not we boxed out on each shot, whether or not we or treated each play as if it was dire, whether or not we approached each game with optimism and fortitude.

Similarly, I could not control whether or not I contracted leukemia, how my body handled the treatments, or how long it took me to beat cancer. But I could control the little things: whether or not I approached each day from a standpoint of positivity or negativity, whether or not I entered each situation with a strong or weak mentality, whether or not I dwelled on what I didn't have.

This was a part of my game plan: focus on the little things, be patient in the present, and persevere through it all. It was all I could do.

As my recovery ensued, I was pulled deeper into my game plan. With each passing day, I was one step closer to victory.

∽

On October 29, Dr. Voorhees jovially walked into my room and told me that I had gone into molecular remission. Again, because he had been so straightforward with me in delivering bad news, I knew that I could also trust him in delivering good news.

"I'm so excited," I remember him telling me. "This is major, you going into remission so quickly. This is really, really good."

I learned that the biggest challenge for doctors often times was not getting a patient into remission but keeping the person there. For example, I remember a little girl down the hall from me who had gone into remission but then quickly came out of remission. Doctors could get her into remission, but they could not keep her there. The longer a patient remains in remission, the less chance he or she has of getting out of remission.

Then there was Lauren Wilburn, a young woman in her thirties at Lineberger, who couldn't get into remission for the life of her. Doctors tried for a year and a half. They sent her to MD Anderson Cancer Center and to Memorial Sloan Kettering Cancer Center. When she was at Lineberger, I would often sit next to her in the infusion lab and talk to her and her mother for hours. I felt horrible for Lauren. I couldn't imagine how helpless and frustrated she had to have felt. She died on March 20 the following year.

Getting into remission was a vital step.

But staying there was even more important.

- Chapter 10 -
DON'T FIGHT ALONE

"Live. Fight like hell. And when you get too tired to fight, lay down and rest and let somebody else fight for you."
~Stuart Scott (1965–2015), UNC Class of 1987, ESPN sportscaster

On November 7, I was discharged and cleared to return home. I was still extremely weak and sick, but I was excited to be going home nonetheless. It felt like I had been in the hospital for an eternity. I felt very grateful that the chemotherapy process was, for the most part, going as planned.

I certainly wasn't allowed to drive, so Sammy took me to our house. Right when we pulled into the driveway, Maddie, my golden retriever, sensed that I was home and greeted me at the car. Sammy was afraid that Maddie, in her exuberance, would hurt me because I was so frail and sick, so Sammy held Maddie when I opened the passenger side door, preventing her from jumping on top of me. However, it was as if Maddie immediately understood that there was something that wasn't quite right about my health. She slowly and gently climbed up into my lap and began to lick my bald head as if to say, "Mom, what's wrong with you? I will help you. I will fix it."

Already, Maddie was helping me.

∽

The story about Maddie represents so much more. The truth is that from the moment I was diagnosed, both the kind people at Lineberger and my dear friends were doing that exact same thing for me every single day: running out to meet me right where I was and then helping me in whatever way I needed help. Whether I was in the hospital or at home, I was in good, loving hands. I had yet to spend a single second alone since my diagnosis one month before. And I wouldn't throughout the remainder of my treatments.

Being back home and away from Lineberger, removed from the brutality of that initial chemo treatment and my first month in the hospital, gave me ample time to reflect on how amazing the doctors, nurses, and people were at UNC Cancer Care.

What's interesting about the infrastructure at Lineberger is that compassionate care encompasses everything that they do. Whereas some hospital systems seem to divide research (scientists and doctors) and compassionate care (nurses, therapists, and others who work with the patients), one of the cornerstones of Lineberger is marrying the two.

For example, just like most hospitals, Lineberger has different departments: pediatrics, research, surgery, neurology, and medicine. Once a week, however, the doctors, scientists and surgeons from each field—say, those who are working with breast cancer patients or providing research and innovative strategies in their fight against breast cancer—get together and learn from one another, uniting around the common challenge. What this ultimately does is create synergy among the Lineberger staff so they can better serve the patients and also better serve one another. This oneness creates an undeniable spirit of hope around the hospital.

Because Lineberger takes on some of the most difficult cases and therefore unfortunately sees a lot of people pass away, emotional and psychological support for both Lineberger's patients and employees is of utmost importance. I've been told that Lineberger hires people, yes, for their skill, but also for how they fit into the Lineberger family and how they add value to this aspect of compassionate care.

A couple months before I checked into the hospital, a Lineberger breast cancer surgeon named Dr. Keith Amos unexpectedly died, at the mere age of forty-two, from a ruptured aorta when he was on sabbatical in Edinburgh, Scotland. I personally knew Keith as the amazing person he was, and I saw his death shake the Lineberger community. Throughout the grieving process, someone from a different institution commented to Dr. Shelley Earp that he had never seen a group of people who cared so much about each other.

This is just an example of the Lineberger employees' collaborative spirit that seemed to make their love for one another, and the patients under their care, so genuine and profound. In my opinion, it was this undercurrent of love that made Lineberger such a special place. Though I was in the middle of my fight, I felt blessed to be in such good hands.

During this time, however, when I was home, I became less dependent on the doctors and nurses and more dependent on my friends. The doctors would still call me every day, and Claudio would even come to my house to help me work out. Now, instead of walking seventeen laps around the top floor of the hospital, we would walk a two-mile loop on the gravel, wooded roads through my neighborhood out in the country. He continued to lead me through exercises with free weights and resistance bands. But it was my friends who were with me all the time, as I continued to encourage Sammy and Van to keep living their lives.

Beginning with my first month in the hospital, Dianne sent an email out to my closest friends, and they all collaborated on a schedule so I wouldn't spend a second alone. Though many of them didn't know one another, they worked together to help me. There was a waiting list of people wanting to stay with me. In the midst of all this, it was humbling to realize how selfless and caring my friends were. I knew that I had great friends but I never knew how great until I got sick. A friend would come, and she wouldn't leave until the next person arrived. Most of the time, each person would stay with me for multiple days at a time.

At the hospital I was under the careful care of the Lineberger doctors and nurses, but once I returned home, my closest friends became my caretakers. Though my numbers were rising, which allowed me to be released from the hospital, my health was as fickle as could be, sometimes changing by the minute.

Dianne (being a nurse) made a special cookbook that she sent out to everyone since I had neutropenia, a disease caused by chemotherapy that makes your ability to fight infection basically non-existent, thus limiting the kinds of food you can eat. (I could not eat things like restaurant food or raw vegetables.) The book also included information about the importance of keeping a germ-free environment, wearing a mask and gloves when they were around me, and not preparing my food with bare hands. In the book, Dianne also explained the type of chemotherapy I had undergone and its side effects so my friends would be able to identify signs or symptoms, which could indicate areas of concern or problems. On the front of the book, Dianne put a picture of Sammy, Van, and me all holding the Naismith trophy. It was hard to believe that picture had only been taken a couple months before. How things had changed!

While I was at home, as up and down as my days were, as weak as I often felt, two things were consistent: Maddie would lie next to me on the couch and follow me around the house from room to room, as if to watch over me, and my friends were constantly present, which was one of the most humbling things I have ever experienced.

As I've mentioned, because of how my leukemia was weighing on Sammy and Van, one of my goals was to make their lives as normal as possible with their daily activities. They were by my side whenever I needed them, but I tried to lean more on my girlfriends and primary caregivers so that Sammy and Van could live normally.

To be honest, seeing how much people were sacrificing for me—rearranging their schedules, making long drives, and tending directly to my needs—was a little weird at first. I was used to being the one tending to my friends, showing my love for them. I liked giving, not receiving. I liked independence, not dependence. There was a part of me that was a little bit uncomfortable with all they were doing to express their love for me. Who was *I* to have been blessed with such caring friends?

As crazy as this sounds, there was an aspect of it all that was kind of fun, even though I felt miserable. Some of my friends who came to help me were friends I hadn't seen in a long time. As the adage goes, "Make new friends, but keep the old; one is silver and the other gold." It was like a reunion of sorts. My battle with leukemia opened up opportunities to spend time with them. It also opened up an opportunity for my friends to grow closer with one another. Many of them did not know one another because they were from different phases of my life, but they were able to bond over a common cause: my leukemia. Because of my cancer, their friendships deepened.

On top of my best friends' generosity, I continued to receive phone calls, texts, and cards from friends and fans every single day. It was unbelievable. I received constant calls from legendary women's basketball coach Pat Summitt, former North Carolina governor Bev Perdue, ACC commissioner John Swofford, and UNC men's basketball coach Roy Williams. I also received multiple calls from Duke men's basketball coach Mike Krzyzewski, *Good Morning America's* Robin Roberts, and ESPN anchor Stuart Scott.

Stuart had reached out to me multiple times since my diagnosis. I still have a couple of his texts and voicemails on my phone (he died on January 4, 2015 during his third bout with cancer). I always found myself hanging on every word he said when he texted or called. To be honest, I sometimes still listen to the voicemails that he left or reread the texts he sent me. They are inspiring. He was an inspiring man.

"Girl," he would say to me throughout my first treatment, "today you are going to feel like crap, but you can do it. You have to keep fighting, girl. I'm here for you. If you need me, you call me, you text me."

Overall, I was constantly humbled to see how people really cared— whether it was a close friend, a fan, or someone who had a public platform.

When a struggle arises in our lives, it's tempting to think that we can go through it alone. Sometimes a struggle that we endure is simply the byproduct of our fallen world, where things naturally go wrong. Other times a struggle is the byproduct of our own wrongdoing; there are sometimes worldly consequences for our mistakes. Regardless of the struggle, it's vital that we never allow ourselves to think, out of pride, that we can fight alone. You can't do it alone. I certainly couldn't. In her book *Real Moments*, Barbara de Angelis wrote: "Difficult times always create opportunities for you to experience more love in your life." I couldn't agree more.

∽

Success in this life is all about relationships. I was reminded of this reality more than ever when I was dependent on my best friends' diligent care. It was in those broken moments—like when I was lying in my bed and hardly had the strength to eat or lift my head but still had the presence of a friend in my midst—that I realized there is nothing more important in this life than relationships and friendships.

I am an ambitious person, and I love to win. Some of my most memorable seasons consequently involved a lot of winning. As I reflect on my coaching career, however, as rewarding as those ACC titles and national championships were, and as much as I want to continue striving to win ACC titles and national championships, the most lasting, impactful moments with my players have been the broken ones—the "hold the rope" moments and the tearful prayers. Though it is fun to reflect on winning and success, when past players reach out to me, it is usually because of something in their journey that entails some sense of brokenness or pain. This world is not without hardship, and it is in hardship where we need one another the most.

My assistant Jane High recently had a conversation with someone who said something along the lines of, "If something ever happened to me similar to what Coach Hatchell went through, I don't know if my friends or family would be there for me like they were for her." This particular person had invested too much time in her career, chasing after all kinds of worldly pursuits in an attempt to attain status, fame, and financial success. This is a sad reality of some people, but it is never too late to start all over and bring relationships to the forefront of your priorities, or to apologize to those you have wounded.

In our dog-eat-dog, performance-driven country, it is time to redefine the definition of success. Motivational speaker Brian Tracy once said, "Successful people are always looking for opportunities to help others. Unsuccessful people are always asking, 'What's in it for me?'"

Success is about relationships: our relationship with God and our relationships with one another. One of the most beautiful things about relationships with one another is that we can experience God through each other. This was certainly true for me, especially when I returned home. My friends were the hands and feet of Jesus to me. I experienced God's love through their love and care for me.

♋

Being dependent on others was undoubtedly something that was unfamiliar territory for me. What I learned, however, was that suffering presented an opportunity to develop a lifestyle that was marked by thankfulness and gratitude. It is in our sufferings that we are humbled the most and in our vulnerability that we are most open to the care and generosity of others—not because we want to be, but because we have to be. In life's most challenging situations, we are forced, more than at any other time, to find some smidgen of positivity or hope that will light up our souls in their darkest moments. American author William Arthur Ward once said, "Gratitude can transform common days into thanksgivings, turn routine jobs into joy, and change ordinary opportunities into blessings."

It is somewhat easy to adopt a lifestyle of gratitude and positivity when all is going well in our lives. It is much more difficult when it feels like we are walking through the valley of the shadow of death. But if we can somehow find a way to be thankful in the valley, our thinking no longer hinges upon our circumstance. Only then can we begin to develop true contentment in our lives. Contentment is found in our thinking.

One of the things I tried to tell myself each day I awakened, no matter how bad I felt, was this: "Each and every day, I let no one and nothing take my joy away." There was too much to be thankful for to let my joy fall by the wayside.

My friends.

My church.

My biological family.

My basketball family.

My UNC family.

My Lineberger family.

There is always too much to be thankful for in this life to abandon joy. In Philippians 4:11–13 (ESV), Paul writes, "Not that I am speaking of being in need, for I have learned in whatever situation I am to be content. I know how to be brought low, and I know how to abound. In any and every circumstance, I have learned the secret of facing plenty and hunger, abundance and need. I can do all things through Him who strengthens me."

God continued to meet me wherever I was, and He strengthened me through the gift of His people. Thank you, God.

- Chapter 11 -
DISCOVERING PERSPECTIVE IN DISAPPOINTMENT

"If you make every game a life and death proposition, you're going to have problems. For one thing, you'll be dead a lot."
~Dean Smith (1931–2015), UNC men's basketball coach (1961– 1977)

Throughout October and November, doctors continued to scour the Be The Match database to find a match for me. Just because they had decided to probably pursue Plan B (consolidation treatments) did not mean that Plan A could not be reimplemented at any given time. The University of North Carolina also hosted several Be The Match campaigns around campus.

Though I certainly wanted to find a match for myself, what I found most encouraging about the different campaigns was that other lives would inevitably be saved; more people would be added to the registry, making for more matches around the country.

Regardless of whether or not a match was found for me, my recovery was going well. My body had recently regained its strength from the initial treatment, and my numbers rose back to normal within a matter of three weeks. Considering it usually took about a month for a patient's numbers to rise, I took my progression as a very positive sign. I was right on track. Of course, because we were yet to find a match, this meant that I would have to enter the next phase: a series of four consolidation treatments.

Consolidation therapy is used to kill any cancer cells that might be left in the body. The process would be similar to my initial treatment in the hospital: chemo, wait for my body to take its dive, then recover (for these treatments, however, I could recover at home). What excited me most was that if my body continued to recuperate throughout my consolidation treatments as quickly as it did from my initial treatment, I would be on pace to return to my head coaching duties by NCAA tournament time. Just the thought of returning to coaching brought me so much hope and life.

I was readmitted for chemotherapy in mid-November and entered my first consolidation treatment with pep in my step. I figured that my treatments would only get easier from here. There's no way they could get worse, right? I believed the hardest part—the intensity of the "7 and 3" treatment and my body's initial dive—was over. I was ahead of pace. This time I only had to take treatments twice a day before I was given a day off. This cycle continued six times. When it was over, I returned home.

Ten days later, my body bottomed out. Again, this meant that my immune system went flat and that my white blood cells, platelets, and neutrophils once more dropped to zero. And my fight began again.

✼

As my body returned to its unbearably weak state, I had to go through all the regular protocol because the chance for infection is so high. I was on a strict diet, usually wore a mask, and frequently washed my hands with hand sanitizer. Maddie once more could tell that something was not right with me, and she was always at my feet, just wanting to be close to me. She would sleep right by my bed during the evenings or lie next to my feet on the couch during the day. I wasn't supposed to pet her, but I often couldn't help myself. She was too precious. It's hard to say no to those big brown eyes. Each time I touched her, I would wash my hands with hand sanitizer. It wasn't uncommon for me to wash my hands every couple of minutes throughout any given day, just to be safe.

Because my body was so weak, I had to go to Lineberger every forty-eight hours to get platelets and blood. I would usually go on Mondays, Wednesdays, and Fridays. Some of my weakest moments were on Sunday evenings, since I would often go the duration of the weekend without visiting the infusion lab. I particularly remember visiting an empty hospital over Thanksgiving and having to take my treatments in the bone marrow unit because the infusion lab was closed. I was truly dependent on these treatments during this time. Though it was strange to be spending my Thanksgiving in a hospital, I didn't let my spirits get down. I was determined. All I wanted to do was put my leukemia behind me and be back on the court again.

My numbers were expectedly low upon the initial dive. But then another week passed and my numbers were yet to climb back to normal. I actually felt *worse* than I did after the intense initial treatment.

And then another week passed.

And another.

And another.

Before I knew it, mid-December was upon us. In my initial treatment, my numbers returned to normal after only *three* weeks. But *five* weeks after my first consolidation treatment, I still felt horrible. I couldn't begin my second consolidation treatment until my numbers made their climb. And my health was still sometimes changing by the minute—in even more dramatic ways. Throughout any given day, I would suddenly feel lightheaded or nauseous or helpless. Each day was a roller coaster. What was going on? I thought my treatments were supposed to get easier as I went through the process, not more difficult.

This was a curve ball. This was unexpected. This wasn't part of the game plan.

∾

I've been told that the definition of disappointment is unmet expectations.

The fact that it was taking almost *twice* as long to recover from my first consolidation treatment was, to be honest, aggravating and discouraging. My window for a potential postseason return was closing. I still had at least three more consolidation treatments to go.

I tried not to allow the disappointment to linger. The initial sinking feeling actually led to some lifelong truths. First off, though I had a game plan, I learned that in life, and especially in the valleys of life, it's important to realize that the general plan must be that there is no plan. That's called "life." That's what it's like living in this world. When things don't fall into place like you expect them to, it's part of the process. The one thing you can count on in life is that unexpected things *will* happen. Expect life, especially trials, to be unexpected. The only thing about life that is consistent is its inconsistency.

What's interesting about my bout with leukemia—and specifically the frustrations I endured after my first consolidation treatment—is that some of the same things I learned throughout the process of fighting for my life are very applicable to what I am going through right now, as I write this, with the ensuing investigation of the University of North Carolina's academic scandal. Though my lawyers prefer that I speak relatively vaguely on the subject, I feel like it would be a disservice to the reader for me not to mention this situation, considering the timing of this book's release.

We are all affected by things that we have no involvement with or control over. For example, at this stage in the narrative in my bout with leukemia, I couldn't control how quickly my body recovered from the treatments. I couldn't control that my platelets were always low or that I should have already moved on to my second consolidation treatment.

Two years later, during the NCAA's investigation of UNC, I couldn't control that my legacy and reputation were being questioned over something that I had nothing to do with and of which I had no knowledge. I did not know the professor or the administrative assistant who were named in the NCAA allegations. It's difficult for people to be questioning my integrity in a profession I have been in for forty-two years. My name hasn't been mentioned in the investigation, but I am still a victim to it all, suffering the consequences. Regardless, I want to teach my players, and people in general, how to deal with adversity in my handling of each trial that I face.

In both situations, I have learned that perception is not reality. When my body's numbers were struggling to return to normal, my perception of my lack of progress was frustrating and aggravating and confusing. But that didn't mean that I always had to be frustrated or aggravated or confused. In battling cancer, or in going through any kind of strife in life, it is actually quite "normal" to encounter difficulties. Accepting this reality frees us up to venture through life and to not always be rattled or flustered when things do not go our way. Life isn't supposed to always go our way.

Similarly, in having my name attached to the UNC academic scandal, people's questioning and skeptical perception of me did not have to become my reality. I have found it valuable, when things don't go how I wish, to focus on my purpose, not the problem.

No matter how my body reacted to the chemotherapy, I could focus on my purpose rather than dwelling on the problem.

No matter what people said about me in the chaos of the scandal, I could still focus on my purpose rather than trying to eradicate the rumors or micromanage something that I couldn't control.

Yes, the strife can sometimes be difficult to reckon with. When the No. 1 recruiting class in the country enrolled at UNC the year I got leukemia, I believed in the back of my mind that by the time they were juniors or seniors, we might have the best team in the country. Of course, for those of you who do not know the story, two years later, that recruiting class had mostly transferred (probably because of the looming academic scandal at UNC), we had a number of injuries, and we were only playing with six scholarship players during the 2015-16 season. One could argue that if it weren't for my leukemia or the NCAA investigation, two things that I could not control, we might not have lost the No. 1 recruiting class that we had worked so hard to get. We might currently have the best team in the country. But we don't. It has been my philosophy, and it has been proven time and time again, that if a player chooses not to attend UNC or decides to transfer from UNC, it is her loss.

Perception is not reality. Happiness in life can often be boiled down to our ability to accept the things that have not gone how we anticipated or expected. Unmet expectations have the potential to breed long-lasting disappointment and discouragement, but our ability to accept what has gone wrong allows us to press forward through the messiness of life. I have learned to let go of anger and bitterness; it eats you from within. Remember: he or she who angers you controls you, and I choose to let no one and nothing control me.

When it came to my cancer, I could not avoid the reality that I was way behind in my recovery. I drifted from the original game plan for reasons that were beyond my control. I had no idea what was in store for me, but I tried to believe two things: (1) that I could accept what was taking place; and (2) that I could press on and carry with me a healthy perspective on life and the process I was enduring.

∽

As I mentioned, the holiday season was hard that winter because of the disappointment of not being able to stay on schedule with treatments. However, one of the highlights of the Christmas season was when a group of people showed up on my porch one evening, singing Christmas carols.

When I opened the door, I saw several of my girlfriends along with people from my local church, UNC, and our neighborhood—all singing to me. I later found out that this was something my girlfriends had organized to lift my spirits. I was unable to get close to the carolers because of my weak immune system, but I stood on my front porch and enjoyed the experience. At the end of the caroling, I got another surprise when an Elvis impersonator made his way through the crowd and began performing for me. This impersonator was Keith Henderson, who I'm told is one of the top Elvis impersonators in the country. Interestingly, his father owns the Shrunken Head off Franklin Street in Chapel Hill. Keith sang "White Christmas," "Blue Christmas," and a number of hymns with a scarf around his neck (like Elvis so typically did).

Though my recovery was not going as I had hoped, the little things were bringing me joy. As Elvis once said, "Whatever I am, whatever I will become, will be what God has chosen for me."

- Chapter 12 -
YOUR PURPOSE DOES NOT GO AWAY; IT CHANGES

"This is how sad my life is: I got a scar from scratching my chicken pox too much. That's my big scar story. I really have no major scars."
~Lewis Black, UNC Class of 1970, comedian and playwright

At the turn of the year, doctors cleared me to attend my first basketball game of the season: a home game on January 2 against James Madison. To be honest, the entire evening was extremely difficult. It was unlike anything I had experienced before in the arena of basketball.

I was in Carmichael Arena, where my life's work of coaching was fleshed out each and every day, whether in my office, in the weight room, or down on the court for practice or a game. Yet instead of coaching on the sidelines, I found myself sneaking into the arena through the back entrance, wearing a mask and gloves, avoiding contact with anyone (for medical reasons), and sitting up in a sideline-television platform next to John Strader, Dr. Voorhees' physician assistant. It dawned on me that this was the scene I had dreamt about six months before—how this book began.

To be candid, watching that game was really, really hard—especially as someone who was used to being in control in that atmosphere. I was used to being on the sidelines and having a say regarding the game and my team. But on that day, I couldn't even show my face in the locker room, yell out a play, or be a part of the game in any fashion because of my immune system. I felt handcuffed. Quarantined.

My players—my beloved girls—saw me up there on the platform, but I couldn't talk to or interact with them. All I could do was sit up in the shadows with my mask on and wave. To be honest, in those moments, I wished I hadn't even gone to the game. I felt as if I had abandoned my girls. Sure, I knew that I was wrestling with something I couldn't control, but I also knew that this wasn't what they had signed up for either. My assistants, under the direction of my long-time associate head coach Andrew Calder, were doing an exemplary job—I have the best assistants in the world—but still, those girls came to the University of North Carolina to play for me.

That game, more than any other time in my bout with cancer up to that point, made me realize how helpless I was. I felt so isolated, so useless. I felt a sense of worthlessness I had never felt before, like my very presence was hurting my kids' college experience. Why was I even there if I couldn't help anyone or coach anyone?

∽

The person who loses something must eventually come face-to-face with the reality of what he or she has lost. I had lost basketball—my coaching profession—and, more importantly, I'd lost the typical day-to-day relationships with my players that flowed from basketball. And I had no idea when basketball would re-enter my life—or if it would ever re-enter my life again. Had I already coached my last game? It was a dark thought, and at the time, my recovery was not going as planned. If the treatments were going to continue to become more difficult, not getting easier as I originally anticipated, what would the next round of treatment be like? Or the third one? Or the fourth one?

Though the physical effects of my illness were ever-present, the emotional effects of my illness became very real that day at Carmichael. That was the day that I came face-to-face with the reality of what I had lost. The truth is that there had been a coaching void in my life for three months, but it wasn't until I attended that game that all of it became very real.

Sometimes we must move directly through emotional pain if we ever hope to move past it.

It is easy to want to avoid reckoning with what we have lost, but the void lingers and reveals itself in a variety of ways. Sometimes it shows in anger. Sometimes in sadness. Sometimes in bitterness. Whatever the case, the thing we've lost is always there. That's what makes loss so paradoxical.

I didn't choose to attend that game. I only went because I could, and I didn't know when I would be able to attend another game again with my second consolidation treatment on the horizon. But looking back, I realize that it was worth it—and not because being at Carmichael Arena was fun or enjoyable. It helped me to move through the eye of the storm, the crux of the pain. Despite the fact that I had already experienced some of the weakest days in my entire life, attending that game was one of the most torturous things that I had to endure in my fight with leukemia up to that point.

Because of how long it took for my body to recover from my first consolidation treatment, I had finally begun to accept that I probably would not be coaching during the 2013–14 season—my first season not being a head coach since 1973, when I was playing at Carson Newman and coaching the seventh and eighth grade girls basketball team at Talbot Elementary School. Back then, at Talbot, we finished the season 16–4, had three players make All-Conference, and played for the conference championship. After that, I was hooked. I still have a photograph of that team hanging up in my office.

The point is that it had been *forty years* since I had not been the head coach of a basketball team. A profession that I loved, something that didn't even feel like a profession because it was so much fun, so meaningful, so enjoyable, so challenging—*zap*—was gone in an instant.

As I reflect, I think that is one reason why that James Madison game was so difficult: I knew there was no way of attaining what I wanted the most. At least for this year, I had to say goodbye to coaching as I knew it.

Three days later, I was going to attend another game. And maybe I could move through the pain even more.

∽

On January 5 our tenth-ranked Lady Tar Heels were set to face the eighth-ranked Maryland Terrapins in the Atlantic Coast Conference opener. But more than that, it was a meaningful game to me and to Maryland head coach Brenda Frese, because the university was hosting a Be The Match campaign in the concourse of Carmichael Arena. Brenda and her husband Mark Thomas have twin sons, and one of them, Tyler, was diagnosed with leukemia in 2012. Tyler is doing well today, but both parents use every opportunity they can to bring attention to cancer awareness.

In front of a near-sellout Tar Heel crowd, the evening was a beautiful demonstration of how sports, as competitive as it can be, especially between two of the top teams in the country, also has the potential to bring people together for a greater good. Anytime throughout the game, fans could make their way out into the concourse and get their cheeks swabbed for Be The Match.

Again, from a professional standpoint, it was hard and uncomfortable for me to be at the game. I was able to give the team a brief pep talk in my mask and gloves during the pre-game meal at Carmichael, which I was thankful for, but that was as close as I could get to having any sense of control over the outcome of the game. When play started, I sat up on the platform once more and waved to those who tried to get my attention. Again, feelings of isolation and helplessness washed over me occasionally.

At halftime, I asked John Strader if it would be okay for me to say something to the crowd. My request was spur-of-the-moment and was not part of any of UNC's plans for a halftime show or presentation. John was hesitant and cautious but approved. I think he knew how agonizing it was for me to sit there and how much this moment would mean to me.

John walked down to the floor with me. I wore my mask and gloves. He wouldn't let me hold the microphone so instead held it for me. When I reached center court, everyone in attendance grew silent. This was my first time saying anything audibly to the Tar Heel fan base since the media luncheon back in October. Since then, I had not done any television or radio interviews. Any quote of mine was taken from a North Carolina press release.

The first thing I did was call Mark Thomas, Coach Frese's husband, to center court. Though opponents on the court, our families were in the fight against leukemia together off the court—and now on the court as well. I do not remember exactly what I said. But I remember encouraging those in attendance to get their cheeks swabbed for Be The Match in the concourse.

"You never know," I told them, "you could save a life tonight. You could save my life tonight. You could save a child like Tyler tonight."

The remainder of the second half, despite it being an ESPNU conference opener against two Top Ten teams, I remember the stands being practically empty because the lobby was full of people sitting on the floor filling out forms and standing in line to participate in Be The Match.

∽

Months before, my primary purpose in life had been what it had been for nearly four decades: to encourage young women and mold them through the art of coaching and the tool of basketball. It was indeed agonizing to sit during those two home games at Carmichael and feel isolated and handcuffed, but looking back, it was also a beautiful dawning of a new purpose and a new platform: to share my story about battling cancer with others.

In venturing through the fight of my life against leukemia, my purpose did not go away; it changed. It was redirected. It expanded.

I once read about a Marine in the Korean War, Oliver Prince Smith, who said, "We're not retreating, we're just advancing in a different direction." Similarly, because of a storm, my story was expanding into new areas beyond the hardwood—into arenas I never expected. Yes, I missed coaching, primarily because those day-to-day interactions offered the potential to change and mold lives for the better. But now, in this phase of my life, there was the potential to *save* lives.

I might not have come to this realization at the time, but in reflection I understand that there couldn't have been a more fitting way for me to step into this new expansion of my story than at Carmichael Arena. Though it occurred in the most unordinary of circumstances—cancer-stricken, unable to do the one thing I loved the most, coach—I see that it was not a curse. It was an opportunity. A blessing.

Could it be true that our tests can actually become testimonies? Could it be true that life's most challenging circumstances actually present an opportunity for us to *expand* our purpose and help people in a *different* way than before?

I might have been forced to sit up on that lonely platform during those games, but it seemed that God was giving me a front-row seat to how He might expand my purpose in this world.

- Chapter 13 -
FINDING JOY IN SUFFERING

"You know when you're young, you think you will always be. As you become more fragile, you reflect and you realize how much comfort can come from the past. Hymns can carry you into the future."
~Andy Griffith (1926–2012), UNC Class of 1949, actor and producer

On January 16, I was readmitted for more chemo, my second consolidation treatment. The strategy was the same as my first. Two-a-day treatments. Day off. Repeat.

After six cycles, I returned home, knowing that my body would take another dive in eight to ten days.

What would it be like this time? Could it possibly be worst than the last?

Most cancer patients do not die from the cancer itself; they pass away because their bodies cannot handle the brutal treatments.

∽

Just as I expected, my body took a dive in ten days. And by dive, I mean plummet. I was getting used to this by now. The cycle. The routine. But it was still difficult. Thank goodness I had my friends and family there to take care of me and Maddie there to comfort me. Through it all, I continued to exercise daily.

A month went by, and what I might have suspected became a reality: it became even *more* difficult for my numbers to rise back up to normal, even more difficult than in my previous consolidation treatment.

Every forty-eight hours, my friends would take me to Lineberger so that I could get platelets and blood. I was almost always the first patient there to be treated. I usually needed platelets. Sometimes I also needed blood. On the days I needed platelets, I was usually there until noon. When I needed blood, I would sometimes be there until as late as five o'clock in the evening.

This dive in particular was worse than the two before. It's interesting how much worse something can get when you're convinced it's already as bad as it can be. One Sunday evening when I was feeling especially low, I was sitting at my kitchen table when I received a call from my dear friend Anne Graham Lotz, who had continued to constantly check up on me throughout my treatments.

"How are you feeling?" she asked me.

"Anne, I feel so weak," I said honestly.

Anne knows me well and understands that I am drawn toward positive thinking, especially when there is tension and strife. I think this is what led her to tell me, "Sylvia, Jesus sang praises to God before He went to the cross, even though He knew what He was about to do."

In saying this, she was referring to Matthew 26:30 and Mark 14:26, two parallel passages that refer to how Jesus led the apostles in a song of worship at Passover, right before His anguish-filled prayer on the Mount of Olives, one of the weakest moments of His life, leading up to His arrest that evening and crucifixion days later.

"So you're telling me that's the attitude I should have?" I asked.

"Yeah," she said.

"Okay, I got it," I said.

Anne's words were a reminder to me that Christ, in His weakness, still sang praises to God, even though He was agonizing over what was about to happen to Him. He knew His time of suffering was coming, but it did not stop Him from singing praises.

I etched these words into my psyche. I was in the middle of fighting for my life, quite possibly the most challenging battle I would ever face, but I could still sing praises. And singing these praises—acknowledging the blessings in my life when all seemed rocky—would strengthen my mentality.

Anne's encouraging and challenging words were a reminder to me that there was a potential to discover a real transcending joy in my suffering and weakness. Not happiness. Happiness is circumstantial. Joy comes from God, who is bigger than our circumstances in this world.

When she said this, I was reminded of my mornings during that first month at Lineberger. At the start of each day a woman on their cleaning staff, Brenda Walker, would come into my room and sing me the words of "His Eye Is on the Sparrow":

Why should I feel discouraged, why should the shadows come
Why should my heart be lonely, and long for heav'n and home
When Jesus is my portion? My constant Friend is He
His eye is on the sparrow, and I know He watches me
His eye is on the sparrow, and I know He watches me

I sing because I'm happy, I sing because I'm free
For His eye is on the sparrow, and I know He watches me

"Let not your heart be troubled," His tender word I hear
And resting on His goodness, I lose my doubts and fears
Though by the path He leadeth, but one step I may see
His eye is on the sparrow, and I know He watches me
His eye is on the sparrow, and I know He watches me .

I sing because I'm happy, I sing because I'm free
For His eye is on the sparrow, and I know He watches me

Some mornings, Ms. Brenda would come in with the receptionist, and they would sing "Every Praise" together. There were a number of mornings when there were three or four people from Lineberger's staff singing "Every Praise" to me in my hospital room.

One day I was in the infusion lab accompanied by my friend, Patsy Davis, when my ankles started itching. My chest started to hurt as well, and I noticed that my wrists were covered in red streaks.

"Look at this," I said to Patsy, showing her my wrists.

"That can't be normal," Patsy said, quickly rising from her chair.

She began frantically walking around the infusion lab, searching for John Strader.

Moments later, John appeared next to me, and when he looked at my wrists, he yelled, "REACTION! REACTION!"

That's when I knew something was wrong.

In an instant, doctors and nurses were injecting Benadryl into my arm. I could feel the coolness of the Benadryl being flushed through my entire body.

Though I do not remember much about that moment, Patsy said that my eyes were big and that I could not stop shaking.

I eventually calmed down, but it was quite the scare. I had never had a reaction in the infusion lab before.

As I would find out, my body had reacted negatively to the blood that was being pumped into my system. I had to undergo an EKG test and an ultrasound on my heart to make sure that there was no long-term damage. Everything was okay, but doctors had no idea why my body had reacted the way it did.

I was afraid that I would have a reaction like that again.

∽

Matthew 10:29–31 states: "Are not two sparrows sold for a penny? Yet not one of them will fall to the ground outside your Father's care. And even the very hairs of your head are all numbered. So don't be afraid; you are worth more than many sparrows."

Jesus seems to intrinsically acknowledge in these verses that there will be times in our lives when we might feel abandoned or worthless or as if God does not care about our difficult situation. If people always felt that God loved them and cared about them, then Jesus would have had no reason to talk about the subject.

But He does address the idea. Because He knows that people feel like they've been abandoned, and He wants them to know that they have not been abandoned. And so He explains how intimate and intricate God's love is for mankind. Sparrows were not a delicacy—two were sold for a penny—yet Jesus says that God knows when a sparrow falls to the ground and even *cares* when a sparrow falls to the ground. If God cares about something as seemingly meaningless and worthless as a sparrow, then surely He cares about mankind, the prize of His creation.

His eye is on the sparrow, and I know He watches me.

∽

One Sunday morning, not long after my talk with Anne, I remember waking up and feeling better than normal, the best I had felt in the recovery from my latest consolidation treatment. Perhaps my body was finally starting to progress. Maybe I was making headway.

By two o'clock in the afternoon, however, I started to feel *horrible*, the worst I had felt in *all* of my recoveries. By early evening, I didn't even have the energy to get up and use the bathroom. I felt dizzy, my chest was hurting, and I was lightheaded. I just needed to get through the night. I was scheduled for blood work early Monday morning. I couldn't believe how weak I felt, especially compared to how the day had begun.

When I went to bed, I was so debilitated that I was hardly conscious. I remember thinking to myself, "I just hope I wake up in the morning."

I closed my eyes thinking that I might die.

How far I had fallen—from waking up three months before feeling as if I was on top of the world to going to bed in January and hoping I would wake up the next morning.

When I slowly opened my eyes the next day, my first thought was, "I'm alive!"

At seven o'clock my friends took me straight to the hospital. I was so weak that I couldn't even walk up the stairs. I needed assistance into the elevator. When we walked into the blood infusion wing, I told the doctors and nurses, "I never thought I'd be so happy to see you guys. I need blood and platelets."

I was told that my numbers were as low as they had ever been. All of this was a part of the process.

∽

All of us, at some time or another, will come face-to-face with the idea of death. For many, it is a scary idea to consider. It epitomizes the unknown. What's interesting is that in some of my most anxious and weakest moments, I felt the most at peace.

In moments like that, when you're hoping to simply wake up in the morning, you realize how small you really are, how little control you have, and how temporary this life is. Our lives are merely a vapor in the wind, as the book of Ecclesiastes says.

There was something freeing about this idea for me, as strange as that might sound. It relinquished the desperation I felt to get better and return to coaching. Seeing my smallness in the grand scheme of things helped release me from the anxiety I sometimes felt about my life being on hold. In realizing that my life was a vapor, I was able to surrender the idea that my cancer was the be-all and end-all of my existence. I could let go of my struggles and give them to God.

Interestingly, in realizing my smallness, I could feel God's smallness as well—His willingness, as the Creator of the universe, to meet *me* right where I was. I knew that God was there with me and that He cared about me, just as Matthew 10:29–31 and the hymn that was sung to me in the hospital indicated. I could feel His Spirit bringing me comfort. Simply knowing that God was there *with* me because He cared about me helped to alleviate some of the anxiety and stress that I felt in my weakness. His eye was on the sparrow, and I knew He was watching me. I was not forgotten. I was not abandoned. He was there with me.

The most accurate picture that we have of God is a suffering Savior dying on a cross, demonstrating that God dared to *be with* and *suffer for* humanity. This idea didn't magically make my numbers rise back to normal, but it brought a transcending peace and understanding to my mind, just enough to keep pressing on and remain optimistic. He was with me. Emmanuel.

- Chapter 14 -
ONE STEP CLOSER

"I firmly believe that in every situation, no matter how difficult,
God extends grace greater than the hardship, and strength and peace
of mind that can lead us to a place higher than where we were
before."
~Andy Griffith (1926–2012), UNC Class of 1949, actor and producer

It took almost two months for my numbers to return to normalcy after my second consolidation treatment. My initial treatment took three weeks of recovery. The next took six. This one took eight. It was easy to see that it was becoming progressively more difficult for my body to recover. My body's organs were becoming weaker. Each round of chemo took its toll. Through it all, the clock kept ticking; the calendar kept turning.

The timing of my third consolidation treatment was only fitting. I was readmitted into Lineberger for chemo merely three days after our women defeated Duke in the final game of the regular season. Just as our team was moving into the postseason, the most important part of the year, I too was entering the final stretch in a series of treatments that became increasingly more vital.

Two treatments down. Two to go. I was halfway done, but this felt like the postseason. It was time to see what I was made of.

∞

We always tell our players that the season begins all over again during the postseason. No matter how successful the regular season, no matter how dismal, everything starts over again when the ACC tournament comes around. If we had a good regular season, then—no matter our ranking, no matter our previous wins—we had to prove ourselves once more come tournament time. If we had a disappointing regular season, then we had new life come tournament time; no matter our record, no matter our previous losses, we had a chance to make a run.

The success of our postseason always hinged upon our ability as a team to focus on the next game and nothing else. If we had a good season and all we could think about was the chance of winning a national championship, then we were welcoming the possibility of a blindsided defeat by thinking about the future. If we had a bad season and could only think about the frustrations of the year, the chance of a big upset was unlikely because we were entangled in the disappointments of the past. Whatever the case, the present was key. The moment was essential. Nothing else mattered. Without focusing on the moment, the destination never comes. Without intentional focus on the present, the result that you want is hardly attainable.

I have tried to communicate these truths to my players over the years, and now, entering my third consolidation treatment, I found myself communicating these truths to myself. Yes, it had been a disappointing and traumatic season of my life, but all that mattered was the present. The moment. The next game.

∽

Because it was becoming increasingly more difficult for me to recover from the chemo, it also felt increasingly more fulfilling and rewarding when my numbers did return to normal. And then, all of a sudden, right when things were seemingly on the upswing, right when my numbers were back to normal again, I knew I would be zapped and my body would bottom out once more.

In a sense, it was depressing. After all, the climax of each of my recoveries was to return to Lineberger for chemo and knock my system back down again! This had to happen each time to make sure we got rid of all the cancer cells.

To be candid, in my darkest moments and in the valleys of my thinking, it sometimes felt like the chemotherapy was a never-ending process. It had only been five months since I'd been diagnosed with leukemia, but it felt like five years. The process was grueling—not only from a physical and mental standpoint but also because of the sudden change in my lifestyle. I'm convinced that I watched more television during those four months than I had in my entire life. I would watch episode after episode of *The Andy Griffith Show*, a TV series from the sixties that was a childhood favorite of mine. And when I had watched all of them, I would watch two other great shows from the sixties— *Gunsmoke* and *Bonanza*—and then go back and rewatch *The Andy Griffith Show*. Today, I think I can quote every episode. I wasn't looking forward to returning to this idleness. But it was necessary. It was part of the process.

As I entered my third consolidation treatment, I reminded myself that all of this—the chemo, the grueling recovery, and the return to chemo—was part of the process. As miserable as I sometimes physically felt, I still had a life to live, a story to tell, and a team to coach!

∽

At the end of the day, through it all, I knew I could return to this reality: I was one step closer to being back on the court again. During my recoveries, no matter how badly I felt when I went to bed, I was a day closer to my destination when I awakened. This was the mindset that I had when I entered my third treatment. Of course, I dreaded what the chemo was going to do to my body, but it was necessary, and it would put me one step closer to being back on the court.

Handling my leukemia was a marathon, not a sprint. Life itself is a marathon, not a sprint. Each is difficult. Each is painful. There are plenty of cramps. Hundreds of aches. But as long as I could keep taking step after step after step, I knew that I was moving in the right direction. All that matters is each step, as small as it might be, as painful as it might be.

In the Bible we are told to be still and know that He is God (Psalm 46:10) and to not worry about tomorrow (Matthew 6:34). Because of God's divine love that extends into our weakest moments, I had no need to fear. No need to worry. Former Temple University head coach John Chaney once said, "The most important day of your life is today. This very minute is the most important of your life. You must win this minute. You must win this day. And tomorrow will take care of itself."

As hard as it was to not look ahead with worry and anxiety or look behind with regret for all the coaching time I had missed, I knew I had to stay in the present. I had to focus on each step. With each step, I was closer to the finish line and my return to coaching.

Chapter 15

FINDING HOPE IN THE VALLEY

"I think if there's a great depression there might be some hope."
~Lawrence Ferlinghetti, UNC Class of 1941, poet and painter

My first day at Lineberger for my third consolidation treatment was on March 6, the same day as UNC's first ACC tournament game. I watched the ACC tournament in the hospital while chemo was being pumped into my body through my double port.

Each game was a nail-biter. Our girls defeated Wake Forest 69–65, Maryland 73–70, and lost to Duke in the semifinals 66–61, unable to complete the sweep over our rival.

Our girls had two weeks to prepare for the NCAA tournament.

And I had ten days before my body would take yet another dive.

∽

My body bottomed out once more.

White blood cell count: 0.

Neutrophils: 0.

Platelets: close to 0.

How long would my recovery take this time?

Though I felt horrible, I clung to something my doctors mentioned to me when I was readmitted for chemo: that if my numbers began to rise at a reasonable fashion, they might let me sit on the bench with my team during the Final Four in Nashville, Tennessee. I knew this was unlikely considering how long my other recoveries had taken, but the mere thought of once more sitting on the bench with my team was enough to bring a great deal of hope into my life.

This time around, when my body felt frail and when I went to bed feeling as if I was on the cusp of eternity, I would envision myself sitting on the bench with my team at the Final Four. Just knowing that this was a possibility helped me press forward and keep fighting. This is what hope does. It keeps you going. The more difficult a situation, the greater the possibility of experiencing the fullness of hope.

Our girls barely defeated UT Martin in the first round, 60–58. Two days later, we defeated Michigan State, 62–53, to advance to the Sweet Sixteen. My numbers had yet to start rising, but I held onto the hope that they would.

Throughout the tournament, I continued exercising, watching practice on my iPad (as I had been doing all year), and communicating with the players and coaches all that I could. Watching them on my television at home during my dive brought me so much strength. More than anything, it was a healthy distraction from my physical ailments. Though sports can very easily become a god in our culture, it can also be a beautiful distraction from the inevitable difficulties of life.

Leading up to each tournament game, many of my players would text me or call me and tell me that they wanted to win for me. These conversations were a reflection of how the entire year had been. Though I was supposed to be my players' backbone, they were my backbone. Though I was supposed to be encouraging them, they were encouraging me. Though I was supposed to be guiding them as they dealt with life's hardships, here they were, guiding and helping me.

In the end, our women didn't make it to the Final Four. They defeated South Carolina 65–58 to advance to the Elite Eight but unfortunately fell to Stanford 74–65 two days later. Even if they had made it to the Final Four, I don't think I would have been able to go. My body was taking a beating from my most recent dive, which was unlike any other dive before.

I mentioned earlier that there was one night after my second consolidation treatment when I went to bed believing that there was a good possibility that I might not wake up in the morning. Following my latest treatment, there were several nights like this. Though I remember watching the NCAA tournament, I cannot recall the specifics because this phase of my life was very much a blur. Sometimes I would even fall asleep during the games, which, for anyone who knows me, kind of speaks for itself.

When our season came to an end, it was interesting to reflect upon the year. An entire season had gone by, and I was yet to return to the sidelines. The coaching lifestyle I once knew seemed so foreign, so far away. I was far removed from my dream job. Instead, I was in the middle of fighting for my life. It's funny how you don't realize what you have until it's gone—until it is stripped away.

∞

This particular recovery was very much a "two steps forward, one step back" sort of process, but with the help and support of my friends, I continued to press on. My girlfriends continued taking me into Lineberger every forty-eight hours to the infusion lab, and I found myself often times staying at Lineberger until five in the evening to get my numbers stable. Whereas in the past I mostly just needed platelets, now I needed both almost every time I went into Lineberger. What was happening to my body?

As we entered April, my numbers *finally* began to slowly rise. On the days when I would find out that my numbers were going up, even in the slightest sense, I admit that it was an emotional high, almost like winning a big-time conference game. I tried to relish these moments and celebrate them.

When one is moving through a difficult trial, it is necessary to celebrate the smallest things. I think I naturally found myself gravitating toward these tiny joys, as an optimist, because the overall situation was so dark and oppressive. These small progressions were enough to help me maintain some sort of emotional equilibrium. I could focus on a sliver of positivity and allow it to expand in my mind. This mental exercise always seemed to render up an element of hope within me. It wasn't always easy for me to focus on positivity, and I recognize that this is the greatest challenge for most people today. But it is essential, because hope is the very lifeline to a weary soul and bedraggled mind.

Just the other day, a friend of mine sent me a devotional from a Franciscan friar and author named Richard Rohr. The devotional discussed how neuroscience has proved that the brain has a negative bias. Rohr said that a psychologist friend of his once compared our negative and critical thoughts to Velcro (sticking and holding) and our positive and joyful thoughts to Teflon (sliding away). Rohr challenged his readers to adopt a spiritual practice of deliberately holding onto positive thoughts and constantly monitoring our negative thoughts.

In my own situation, I certainly found this to be true, especially in my painstaking recovery from my third consolidation treatment. Again, I could not control how my body reacted, but I could control my thinking. Even if the positive news in my life came in the form of a minimal rise in my blood numbers, it was enough hope for me to latch onto. It was enough for me to focus on while at home between hospital visits.

∽

That spring, I remember frequently going half a mile down the road and visiting my neighbor Iris Tilley's house, which was located on several acres of farmland. Iris would take rescue animals—donkeys, llamas, horses, cows, and goats—and nurture them in their decrepit states. Most of them were old and beat-up.

One of these animals was a scruffy, little donkey named Maybelline. She had a long, pointed face and dark gray, mangy fur. She had deformed hooves and would walk with sort of a limp, as if she was crippled. There was nothing attractive about that donkey. She was by far the ugliest animal in the barnyard.

For whatever reason, I felt strangely attracted to Maybelline. Several times a week, whichever caregiver was staying with me at the time would drive me over to the farm, and upon pulling up, I would lower my window and yell, "Maybelline!" Her ears would perk up, she would raise her head, and she would let out a loud, "Hee-haw!" upon seeing me. Then she would limp up to the fence. Often times, I would get out and feed her a carrot and pet her.

I just loved that little donkey. I think she loved me too.

I think I identified with Maybelline because we were both outcasts. She was the outcast of all the other animals, and because I had leukemia and felt so restricted all the time, I felt like an outcast too.

Seeing Maybelline throughout the week honestly brought me so much joy. And joy always brings with it an element of hope—even in the simplest of things.

Life seems to be like this, doesn't it? Sometimes nothing in our lives looks like we expect it to look; yet when the big things in our lives lack clarity, we are still challenged to find hope and joy in the little things.

For me during this time, it was the possibility of sitting on the bench at the Final Four, or experiencing the rush of excitement when my numbers rose, or visiting the farm throughout the week and saying hello to my friend Maybelline. As small as these things might seem, it is the most tangible element of hope that I have ever felt. Because I needed hope more than ever before.

- Chapter 16 -
WRECKAGE

*"Our old ordinary means nothing here, and we know already, the
ordinary that this is—and is—."*
~Claudia Emerson (1957–2014) from her book *Impossible Bottle*
(2015), UNC Greensboro MFA (1991)

Ironically, one of the first things that I did in the coaching realm
upon the completion of our season was to sit down with one of my star
freshman recruits and her mother as they told me about her desire to
transfer to a different school.

To be honest, even though my numbers were starting to rise, I probably shouldn't have gone. I was still extremely weak. But part of me
still hoped that my presence and power of persuasion might be able to
change her mind. "I haven't had the chance to coach you," I told her. "I
could not control that I was out this year with leukemia. Just give me
an opportunity to be your coach."

But the die had already been cast. She was leaving.

I am not making excuses here, but this was one of the many exam-
ples of how my leukemia left a mark. With all the thousands of people
who were fighting for me and praying for me, it breaks my heart to
say that there were a few opposing coaches and schools who used my
medical situation against me, especially when it came to recruits. How
low can a person stoop to use a medical situation against a person who
is fighting for her life?

The scene in my office was a reminder of the damage that had been
done from being out for an entire season. Maybe she would have trans-

ferred anyway. Then again, maybe she wouldn't have.

Tears were shed. By all of us. Not only did I feel like I could help her a lot as a person and as a player, but she was also a cornerstone for the future of our program.

The scene in my office was a vivid metaphor for the season. It began with my cancer diagnosis. It ended with this. By the end of the meeting, I remember that my chest was in pain because I wanted to be a part of her life and had not yet had the opportunity. No matter what, I still loved and cared for her and her future.

∞

By mid-April my numbers were finally beginning to return to normal. Assuming that they continued to climb, that meant that my fourth and final consolidation treatment was on the horizon. To be honest, I dreaded that final treatment. I had no idea how my body would handle it considering the toll the chemo had taken on my body over the last six months. I did not feel like my body had anything left to give.

On April 17, I had an appointment with Dr. Voorhees to analyze my progress and evaluate the next step. Dr. Voorhees told me that he had talked with his team and that people all over the world had evaluated my case. They all agreed that I had done enough. My numbers were taking longer and longer to rise back up; it was obvious that the chemo's long-term effects on my organs was substantial.

"I'm not sure if your body can handle another treatment," Dr. Voorhees said. "I'm not sure if you will survive."

I believed that he was right. The cancer was gone, and the treatments had worked. My body could start healing and getting strong again.

Dr. Voorhees told me that I could start doing things as I felt like doing them and could begin transitioning back into normal life. I was still extremely weak, but he said that I could begin re-acclimating myself to my previous lifestyle. Dr. Voorhees declared that my treatments were over.

Obviously this was a great day for me. This was the news I had been waiting for since I had been diagnosed in October. I had anxiously awaited this day, when doctors would tell me that I could return to what I loved. It had been a long time coming. I could start coaching again.

Though this most recent news was a huge relief to me, there was still the lingering question in my mind and in the doctors' minds: Had we done enough? Originally, they wanted me to do four consolidation treatments. I had completed three. But my team of doctors thought that three treatments, along with the fact that I had gone into remission so quickly, were all very good signs that we had done enough and that the cancer would not return.

Yes, there were still some unknowns; but the answers would come in time. Doctors said that for a person my age, there was a high probability that AML would be defeated if it did not return within three years after the first chemotherapy treatment. For me, that would be October 2016. Doctors told me that it would take five years for them to officially label me as "cured." That would be October 2018. I say all of this because, as happy as I was to be done with my treatments (and hopefully be done with them forever), I would have blood work every month and a bone marrow biopsy every six months until 2018.

Whatever the case, I felt tremendous relief when I left Lineberger that day. I was done with my treatments. I was done with the grueling recoveries. I was done going to bed in the evenings praying that I would wake up in the morning. That hellish phase of my life was over. It was finally over. Praise God.

∽

I knew when my doctors cleared me to start making the transition back to my normal coaching life that I had a long way to go. As April and May went by, I realized that I wouldn't be returning to true normalcy for a long, long time; instead, the idea of once more stepping into a new normal was reinforced. I am a goal-oriented person and a visionary. When I returned to work, I was ready to launch back into the chase, into building a program, and even into making up for the time I had missed. This ambition, however, could not be fulfilled in the slightest bit.

Because my doctors told me that I could return to my former coaching lifestyle, I think I assumed that my life would go back to normal. I no longer had to wear a mask. I could come into work more frequently. I no longer needed my girlfriends to take care of me. I could drive from place to place. I soon realized, however, that I was *far* from normal. I was not myself.

At first, I ignorantly tried to dive full-fledge back into coaching. When I felt tired or weak, I would try to suppress the feelings, ignore them, and adopt some of the same principles I applied to my workouts in the gym over the years. Push through the pain. Ignore the weakness that you feel. Press on. Fight through.

This, however, often backfired on me. There were days—moments—when I would start to feel good. Then I would work too hard, overdo it, and exhaust myself. I originally believed that my doctors' clearance would allow me to flip the light switch back on again; instead, it was like turning on a really slow dimmer.

Now, more than ever, I realized that the process I was enduring was a marathon, not a sprint. It dawned on me that just because more chemotherapy was no longer on the horizon, it did not mean I had crossed the finish line. Now, in fact, it was even more difficult. I was in the final five miles of this marathon, the most painful miles of all because of what my body had previously endured. Attempting to sprint with approximately one fifth of the race to go was futile and illogical. Combining my physical weakness with the usual stresses associated with the coaching lifestyle made me even more exhausted.

I learned the hard way that I couldn't jump back into the coaching lifestyle as I knew it. Before my chemo treatments, I only needed six hours of sleep per night. Now I needed eight to ten hours of sleep or I felt completely weak and worthless. On top of that, I had to take a nap every two hours. If I went several hours without taking a nap, I would once again begin to feel extremely weak and unable to function. It was almost as if my body had returned to the state of infancy. I had to sleep and eat constantly. While a baby might get cranky if he or she is tired or hungry, my body would just shut down when I was tired or hungry.

Once again I felt like God was teaching me something about perseverance and patience. Now that I *was* cleared to return to my normal life, I couldn't live my normal life the way I expected to live my normal life—not yet, at least. This was my new normal for the time being. And I had to be okay with that.

When someone experiences a traumatic or life-changing hardship, the person who is most affected by the trial must eventually step into a new normal and take note of the wreckage. Sometimes this can be more difficult than enduring the disaster itself. During the disaster, you are merely coping with chaos, trying to survive, and hoping to make it another day. Once the storm settles, however, one is forced to reckon with, and acknowledge, the damage.

Anyone who experiences an element of loss usually cannot fully comprehend the loss in the eye of the storm. During the ensuing storm, they are simply trying to cope. The unsettling realization of their new normal often does not become a reality for quite some time after the storm. This is typically when people need the most comfort and guidance: when they realize that their life has drastically changed without that person they were used to seeing or that thing they were used to having or that life they were used to living.

Once again, that spring I found myself at a mental crossroads: I could either accept my new normal or I could dwell on its imperfections. I could either accept "what is" or spend my time thinking about "what is not."

As I approached the finish line, I was determined not to let this wake-up call turn my world upside down. Instead, I would make adjustments. I would listen to my body, and I would eat and sleep when my body was telling me to eat or sleep—even if it was inconvenient, even if my new normal was a reality that I hadn't expected.

What's funny about the idea of normal is that, really, who determines what is or isn't normal? What one person thinks is normal, another person thinks is extreme. What one person thinks is extreme, another person thinks is normal. I know two things to be "normal" in this life: one, that things will go wrong in this fallen world; and two, that God's love is unconditional through it all.

When things *do* go wrong, I'm constantly reminded that I can become a vessel in the unexpected. It was tempting to say "I'm a victim" when I couldn't return to coaching as I knew it or when I didn't know when I would return to coaching as I knew it, but instead I chose to say, "What I'm going through is a privilege."

It was indeed frustrating to not be able to flip the switch early that offseason, to not have the energy to work my job like I was used to, but I reminded myself that God was at work. He is always at work. Because of something that had gone wrong in my life—my health, an aspect I had no control over—I held onto the belief and hope that God would use me as a channel to encourage others. In this sense, my new normal was actually something I could look forward to.

- Chapter 17 -
A BROKEN STORY CAN BE A BLESSING FOR OTHERS

"My attitude is that if you push me towards something that you think is a weakness, then I will turn that perceived weakness into a strength."
~Michael Jordan, UNC Class of 1986

Throughout the ensuing offseason, I continued to regain my strength. Ever so slowly, I was beginning to feel like my normal self again—more and more. I continued to learn patience and perseverance, the themes of the year.

As I returned to work and once again became visible in the community—no longer quarantined within the walls of my home—something else began to happen. Broken, hurting people—many of whom had in some way been affected by cancer—began to confide in me. Now that I was actually accessible, it was as if my story was attracting an entirely different group of people. It did not take long for me to realize something: because of the latest chapter in my story, I had credibility that allowed me not only to provide people with hope and encouragement but also to *be there* for them during their trials.

I have heard it said that you can only lead people as far as you have gone yourself. Just as it is difficult to coach basketball if you have no knowledge of the game or of coaching, it is also difficult to relate to someone who is having thoughts of death if you have never been on the cusp of dying. Because I had been so broken, I attracted brokenness. Because I had fought such a severe form of cancer, people felt comfortable leaning on me and opening up to me in the heaviness of their emotions or gravity of the trauma. Before I had been diagnosed with AML, I still tried to encourage people, but now it seemed to mean more because they knew that I too had ventured into the depths.

Almost every day, there was a new situation or opportunity to encourage someone—whether it was an email from a stranger or a call from Lineberger about coming over to the hospital to talk with someone. God was taking my story into the fragile situations of others and comforting them with it. Suddenly I was more relatable to people who were in the most delicate and vulnerable of positions. Weak people. Hurting people. People who needed hope in the present. People who were fearful of the future. People who, like me, needed to be strengthened in their weakness and loved in their hurt.

This avenue of ministry and influence was new for me. Not that people never leaned on me before, but now, having gone through what I had gone through, people—strangers, even—were actually attracted to me and depended on me. All because I had battled AML. Because of the trials I had endured, my purpose had indeed expanded. My ability to influence others had broadened. God was now turning my brokenness into a blessing for others. It was humbling to consider that God would use me in such a way.

Never do I want to relive that horrible phase of my life, but I am thankful for it—simply because it has opened up opportunities for me to help others. The most meaningful thing we can do in this life is to help someone else. And I was beginning to discover that being able to help others and meet them where they were in turn also blessed me. Here are a couple of those stories…

∽

I've always believed that givers gain.

When my extended family found out back in the fall of 2013 that I had leukemia and that doctors were looking for a bone marrow match for me, many of them took the initiative to get their cheeks swabbed for Be The Match.

As you know, doctors didn't find a match for me; two years later, however, one of my distant cousin's sons, a young man named Zac Gooch who had been swabbed for me, found out that he was a perfect match for a twenty-two-year-old male with a rare blood disease called myelodysplastic syndrome (MDS).

As he was living in Florida at the time, Zac didn't tell any of his family in North Carolina about his selfless agreement to be a patient's marrow donor, but he did tell his girlfriend that he had a surprise for her and flew her down to Florida. Upon arriving in the Sunshine State, she thought that he was going to take her on a fishing trip (their favorite adventure). Instead, he told her over lunch that he was undergoing surgery the next day to donate his bone marrow and that they would be heading to the hospital in thirty minutes for some preliminary tests. She was shocked but also amazed by what he was going to do.

After his bone marrow donation the next day, he called his parents from the recovery room to fill them in on what he had done. He had just given the gift of life. This might not have ever happened had I not been diagnosed with leukemia. Before his mother hung up the phone, she said to him, "I've never been so proud of you in my life."

∽

Then there's Jasmine DeBerry.

Jasmine played for Wingate University's women's basketball team under head coach Ann Hancock, who was on our UNC staff at Chapel Hill for eight seasons (from 1992–2000). When Coach Hancock found out that I had leukemia, she began hosting Be The Match campaigns at women's basketball games at Wingate. Jasmine found out during the summer of 2014 that she was a match for a nine-year-old girl in New York with Sickle Cell Anemia.

One day, during the 2014 offseason, Anne gave me a call.

"Coach," Anne said, "I just wanted to let you know that I have a player on my team named Jasmine DeBerry who was a match for a little girl up in New York."

"Jasmine DeBerry?" I said, recognizing the name. "I know Jasmine. She was one of the regulars at our summer camps at UNC when she was little."

"She has always looked up to you, Coach," Ann said. "And she wants you to know that she is going to do the procedure for the little girl, yes, but also for you."

I was overcome with emotion. It came at a time when I was restless to be one hundred percent once more and coach like I used to. Instead

I was faltering through each day, unable to function without sleeping or eating every few hours.

That night I told Sammy, "If one person's life is saved because of what I had to go through this past year, then all of it was worth it."

∽

Those are only a couple of stories. Seriously, it would take another book to share with you every blessing I have personally seen from the brokenness I experienced. I am not exaggerating when I say that just about every day there is an opportunity that arises for me to help someone—and this can be traced back to my bout with leukemia. It has been unbelievable. Whether it's hearing about a match that was made through a Be The Match campaign or being able to connect someone with the brilliant people at Lineberger or visiting Lineberger to encourage a patient or talking to someone at a basketball game who is in the middle of a personal storm, the message that has clearly been communicated to me is that God will turn this pain into something good for others. I count it a blessing to be a part of His plan in this world.

Though that year was difficult for me, it has allowed me to help bring hope to others who are going through something similar.

In this sense, my cancer was a blessing.

Though a perfect bone marrow match was never found for me, other lives have been saved because of matches that were made through Be The Match campaigns that were done in my name.

In this sense, my cancer was a blessing.

Though I have yet to finish the memoir I was working on before I was diagnosed with leukemia, this book—one that can help others discover their inner strength in whatever trial they are enduring—was published instead.

In this sense, my cancer was a blessing.

Though cancer almost took my own life, it has also allowed me to share my life in a more profound way with others. I feel like I have gone from being a Christian to being a disciple.

In this sense, my cancer was a blessing.

Each day I am more and more convinced that this is true: my cancer will always be a blessing.

∽

I have learned by now that life hardly ever looks like you expect it to look. And when there are unmet expectations in your life, you can either wallow in disappointment or allow your purpose in this life to expand into areas that you might not have ever expected. Life is never easy. There are always challenges. It is always messy. But God can also take this messiness—our stories—and turn them into messages and blessings for others.

It doesn't necessarily make things in this life any easier or explainable or okay, but I *can* say that I have experienced transcendent meaning in this life in being able to help people in their depths. There is nothing more valuable in this life than meeting people where they are at, coming alongside them, and helping them feel loved and encouraged in their struggle.

In his book *Quiet Strength*, Hall of Fame football coach Tony Dungy writes, "God's definition of success is really one of significance—the significant difference our lives can make in the lives of others. This significance doesn't show up in win-loss records, long resumés, or the trophies gathering dust on our mantels. It's found in the hearts and lives of those we've come across who are in some way better because of the way we lived."

To be honest, whenever I go over to Lineberger today to visit the staff or encourage a patient, I still have flashbacks, especially when I walk through those same halls. I don't know if I will ever be able to adequately process the pain and trauma from those horrendous months, but I *can* say that—though I hope to never have to relive anything like that—I am grateful for how that period of my life opened up doors for me to relate to people.

God can turn a personal trial into something that blesses the lives of others. And this does not necessitate a happy ending. As I write this, I am still not officially "cured" (doctors do not use the word "cured" until a patient has been cancer-free for at least five years). At the same time, I also recognize that many have not been as fortunate as me. There are many who cannot physically handle the treatments—many who have died too young. I will not attempt to explain this, because tragedy and loss are unexplainable. I can only speak from experience. I am thankful for my cancer because it has allowed me to relate to others, and, in doing so, meet them where they are and give them hope.

Read almost any book of the Bible, and you will find that not one protagonist in any story had it easy. Moses left his cushy life as royalty, as a member of Pharaoh's family, and, amidst much anguish and turmoil, he led the Hebrew people out of slavery. Job lost everything he owned. The prophets lived in radical discomfort to convey truths to God's people. Jesus died on the cross before rising again. Most of Christ's apostles died while sharing the gospel.

Yet these are the stories we are drawn to—stories with real pain and real hurt. And all of these stories have something in common: each person was fueled by a transcendent purpose in this life—a purpose that made death lose its sting. The pain will never be explained, but it can be used for the good of others. And this is enough for me.

- Chapter 18 -
RAINBOWS IN THE DEAN DOME

*"Peace fell upon her spirit. Strong comfort and assurance bathed her
whole being. Life was so solid and splendid, and so good."*
~Thomas Wolfe (1900-1938), Class of 1920, novelist

On October 5, 2014, I stood in the tunnel at the Dean Dome,
about to be introduced at the University of North Carolina's annual
"Late Night with Roy," a pep rally for the upcoming men's and women's
basketball seasons. The event is always a lot of fun. It's great for the students and fans, but it's also a nice, exciting transition into the season.
Each "Late Night With Roy" is an anticipatory time, as we look ahead
to the season and dream of what we might accomplish.

Standing in the tunnel, it was interesting to consider that a little over
a year before, I had been living on Cloud 9, having just been inducted
into the Hall of Fame and entering the year with the top recruiting class
in the country. So much promise. So much hope. Not much later, of
course—right before the start of the season—I learned that I had acute
myeloid leukemia, and my life changed.

When you are blindsided by life, you will inevitably change as
well—either for the better or for the worse. We have to choose to allow
change to make us better. It's a choice. After having come so close to the
pull of death, I felt such a deep sense of gratitude for simply being alive.
The things that used to irritate me no longer seemed to irritate me. The
things that used to affect my moods no longer held any weight. Each
moment was seemingly filled with new opportunity. Each day felt like
a glorious blessing. All felt more sacred and beautiful than ever before.

On top of that, I was even more passionate about coaching, more fired up to win, and more determined than ever to make up for lost time. I felt that, at age sixty-two, I was more competitive and hungry than ever before. I had been given a second chance at life.

From the tunnel that evening, all I could see was the hardwood court and a sea of rainbow-colored glow sticks flashing in the packed-out Dean Dome crowd. It was beautiful: layer upon layer of multi-colored beams, creating the most spectacular light show I'd ever seen.

I was reminded that it takes a storm—a rain shower—for a rainbow to finally appear. The rainbow is a reminder that life is not easy; it can be filled with dark clouds and torrential downpours, but it can also be beautiful. It can also be colorful and vibrant. It was only fitting that I could see hundreds of flashing rainbows in the crowd as I stood in the tunnel.

Each time I see a rainbow, I am reminded of God's promise that we are told about in Genesis 9, following the flood. The rainbow is a symbol of God's promise to forever show His love and favor to humanity. The symbol He displayed in the sky did not mean that this life would not be hard or that something as grim as cancer would always be defeated. But it did mean that He wasn't far away in the chaos. He was always there to wrap us in His love.

After all our players were introduced, my name was announced. I began to walk through the tunnel as the announcer read off a list of my coaching accolades; however, not even the phrase "Naismith Hall of Fame member" sounded as good next to my name as his final descriptor:

"Cancer-free."

I walked out onto the center court.

The noise was so loud that for a second I thought UNC had just hit a winning buzzer-beater against Duke. Several people would later tell me that it was the loudest they had ever heard the Dean Dome.

My team ran toward me and surrounded me and lifted me up, just as Love did all along.

- AFTERWORD -

"As soon as you try to describe a close friendship, it loses something."
~Dean Smith (1931–2015), UNC men's basketball coach (1961–
1977)

Throughout the course of the 2014–15 season, I often found myself reflecting on the year before. Because the year had been emotionally traumatic and physically exhausting, it took time to mentally process all that had transpired. When I visited Lineberger, I had flashbacks. It was not uncommon for me to suddenly remember something from my bout with cancer over the course of any given day. There were some things that I could not eat or drink because of the memories associated with their taste.

The point is that I was no longer merely trying to cope while being tossed in the chaos like the year before. No longer was my mind in a blurry haze. The fog was lifted. I no longer had chemo brain. I could dive back into coaching, and as fulfilling as this was, my return to normalcy also allowed me to see how abnormal the year before had been.

In this reflection I was once again humbled by everyone's loving support for me during that hellish year—from the knowledgeable and caring people at Lineberger, to the supportive people at UNC, to my amazing family, and to my ever-present friends.

As I thought about my friends, I was reminded of an episode of *The Andy Griffith Show* in which Andy wakes Gomer from his sleep to put out a small fire at the filling station, which saves Gomer's life. The remainder of the episode, Gomer does everything he possibly can to repay Andy. Gomer's ridiculous attempts are futile; he realizes that there is no way that he can possibly repay someone for saving his life. But he keeps trying anyway. Andy, who becomes somewhat annoyed, decides to stage a scene so that Gomer can "save" Andy's life and feel as if he had repaid him.

I was Gomer.

My friends were Andy.

I wanted to repay them, but I had no idea how. Ultimately, I knew that it was impossible to repay them. I simply had to accept their love. It is impossible to adequately repay someone for saving your life.

I tried to repay them anyway. I wanted them to know how thankful I was for them. So, heading into the summer, I decided to host a ten-day vacation for these friends, all female, in North Myrtle Beach. It had already been a fulfilling year. Our women's team had gone 26–9 overall, 10–6 in the ACC, and had advanced to the Sweet Sixteen in the NCAA tournament. It was a good step in the right direction for our program and a beautiful return for me personally to coaching. But the reality is that I never would have been able to return to coaching to begin with if it wasn't for the support of my friends the season before. A beach trip with my best friends was only fitting.

I invited all the women who had so delicately cared for me throughout the previous season. All I wanted to do was shower them with my love and appreciation after all they had done for me. I looked forward to the retreat with great anticipation because the more I reflected, the more I was dying to give back in some way. Sammy, who was tremendously supportive of my girls weekend, remained in Chapel Hill.

What also made the vacation exciting was that I would host the retreat at my family's brand new beachfront home in North Myrtle Beach—a six-bedroom, five-bathroom home right off Ocean Boulevard. The three-story house was constructed entirely with Carolina blue paneling, and on both the front and backside of the house were wooden, hand-carved signs with paintings of two beach chairs, an umbrella and a golden retriever. On each sign were the words "Blue Heaven," the name I gave to the house.

Sammy and I had started building the house before I was diagnosed with leukemia. We had owned a smaller beach house in North Myrtle for years, but we were looking to invest in another rental property. We decided to pull the trigger on the decision around the time I was inducted into the Naismith Hall of Fame. Though the construction of this new house came to a halt when I was diagnosed, it resumed when I returned home and continued throughout the 2014–15 season. During my recoveries from my consolidation treatments, I spent a lot of time flipping through architecture and interior design books. Doing so kept me distracted. And in many ways, it kept me thinking about something positive: the beach, one of my favorite places in the world.

In my depths, I would often times quiet my mind and picture myself either relaxing in the mountains on the porch of our cabin or walking on the beach with Maddie. It was a mental and meditative exercise that always seemed to bring me a great deal of peace and hope for the future. I couldn't wait to be back in the mountains or at the beach again.

And now, at the end of May, it was as if all was new. I was returning to the beach with a new perspective, having been on the cusp of death a little over a year before. Summer was on the horizon. And even the house was brand new, as we were Blue Heaven's first visitors.

∞

Even more special than being at the beach was the fact that my best friends in the world kept arriving throughout that first day, one by one. Twenty of them. Friends from all different phases of my life. All connected through my sickness.

Everything became more tangible. If it weren't for this collective group, surely I would not have made it through my fight with leukemia. Not only did they care for me; they also kept my spirits up and kept me company in my idle state. Being there at Blue Heaven with those people who I love with all my heart, who all played a part in saving my life, was truly overwhelming. Though not all my friends knew one another, they had at least all heard of one another because of the schedule they used during my treatments. It was almost as if there was an immediate union or oneness among us, simply because of the gravity of my situation. I was bombarded with flashbacks upon seeing some of their faces. In these flashbacks, I was continually overwhelmed by the unconditional love that was displayed to me, over and over again, throughout my fight.

During one of those first days at Blue Heaven, I remember standing on the porch that overlooked the Atlantic Ocean and gathering all of my best friends around. Though I had thanked them each individually many times throughout the course of the year, it was time for me to thank all of them at once, communally.

I tried to speak, but I didn't make it past four words. All I said was, "I could have never..." And then I broke down and began to cry.

∽

One evening I took all my friends to an eclectic restaurant with live music called Martini's. Though North Myrtle Beach is a touristy area, many of the locals spend their time at Martini's, which makes it a special place. A band that I knew was playing that evening, and when they found out why we were all together and what we were celebrating, the band turned the night into a gigantic party for all my girlfriends. We had such a good time.

At one point before dinner, I stood up and tried to once again express how grateful I was. I made it further this time but still got choked up after saying, "I can't thank you enough for what y'all did for me." And before I knew it, I was bawling once again.

I am not a very emotional person—and even when I am emotional, very rarely do I express those emotions—but telling these women how much they meant to me was one of the most difficult things I've ever attempted. I guess that's what unconditional love does sometimes. It breaks you down.

∽

Though I tried to avoid the beach in the mornings and afternoons because of the intensity of the sun on my skin, there were a couple of evenings when I walked down to the beach at dusk with Maddie. Once again, this was a reflective time for me.

It was special to be there with Maddie, who, like my friends, had also seen me in my depths and loved me unconditionally. Upon returning to the hospital after my initial treatment, she had licked my head. Throughout my consolidation treatments, she slept at my feet. And now she was here on the beach, celebrating my recovery.

As odd as this might sound to some people, Maddie was a reflection of the divine to me throughout my fight against leukemia. She was always there. Ever-present. Always comforting. Never judging. She did not expect anything of me. She simply wanted to be with me. She simply wanted to show that she loved me.

Joy in its purest sense is found in unconditional love. I've heard it said before that if you place your identity and purpose in your love for (J)esus, (O)thers and (Y)ourself, you will experience joy. Because joy is found in love, we can always experience some sense of joy, no matter our circumstance.

I was reminded of all this as I walked on the beach with Maddie. Though being there on the beach was especially blissful, I had also experienced joy in my depths. That's because in my depths, I had experienced the love of Christ and the love of others. No matter what else unfolded, I knew that if I kept exploring this love, I would be okay. It would be enough. God's grace would be sufficient.

One evening I stood on the shore, Maddie sitting beside me, and I looked out over the ocean as the sun was setting. I found myself overcome with awe and wonder. Faced with the ocean's magnitude, I was reminded once more of my smallness—how this life is only a vapor in the wind and how the trials of this life will not compare to the joy of eternity. And yet I was also reminded of how the same Creator whose fingerprints were all over the shoreline and the infinite ocean and the expanse of the sky also cared about me with the same intensity that went into creating the masterpiece that I was looking at.

I smiled and reached down to pet Maddie.

Then we walked back up the beach toward Blue Heaven, and I figured I would attempt to thank my friends once more…

∽

And now, as I come to a close, I want to recognize a few of my friends who saved my life:

Dianne Glover: I met you when Sammy and I joined Cresset Baptist Church in 1989. We immediately developed a strong friendship. We are the same age and love the same things: Jesus, beach, beach music, shag dancing, dogs, and a few other things I can't mention. You are a blessing to me in so many ways. Truly a best friend!

Eleanor Burns: You and I met at Francis Marion University in 1975. We immediately enjoyed spending time together and doing a lot of things together, like traveling and listening to music and shag dancing. You are a great cook, and you've been a steadfast friend for more than forty years. Thank you for being there for me throughout my fight.

Phyllis Cooley: Phyllis, you are my older sister by four years. We are very different but very similar in our values, beliefs, work ethic, loyalty and family. You're the backbone of our family, always rock solid, each and every day. You came running when I was diagnosed with AML—a true big sister!

Patsy Davis: My childhood friend from Gastonia Unity Baptist Church. I cannot remember ever not knowing you. Your mother was my favorite Sunday school teacher growing up. Simply put, they don't come any better than Patsy Davis. You are a great Christian and a lifelong friend who makes me apple butter and who is married to one of the greatest guys in the world, Ricky. Thanks for being there for me.

Joy Farley: My Kepley Road neighbor who does so many things to help me. A former ABC network actor in *All My Children* and various commercials, I appreciate how you love UNC women's basketball and take care of me. You also love my golden retriever, Maddie, and Maddie loves you too!

Marylou Garnett: My make-believe little sister—your mom was my best friend and administrative assistant at Francis Marion University. You have always been like my little sister. I videotaped your wedding, and we have always looked after each other. I also give you lots of advice.

Cecilia Grimes: I met you when you started doing etiquette lessons for our team. We immediately had a connection in being Southern and being Baptist. You and I have a true "sister connection" that is hard to explain. We can be together for hours and never say a word, but we have a true connection and a great time, a special chemistry.

Karen Robbins Harper: Our friendship goes all the way back to high school, where your dad was our principal. We spent three summers working together at DANOCA Industries. We worked in a sewing factory for three summers. Trust me; we learned how to work and the value of an education. You're a Tar Heel through and through. You graduated from UNC, where you were a cheerleader, and all three of your children and your husband are also Carolina grads. You're a great gal.

Jane High: "Janie Mae," my dear friend, we met in 1994 when you were my son's kindergarten teacher at Cresset Christian Academy. You are a special lady and friend. You are my administrative assistant, and I could not exist without you. You tell me where to go and what to do. You are a wonderful Christian mother, wife, teacher, and friend. What a lady. The world would be a much better place if we had more people like you.

Christine Kepley: You are my neighbor, who I could not live without. You take care of my flowers and always make the outside of my house look beautiful. You are little lady but you do the work of ten men. You are always showing me how you care in her numerous ways of giving and being a loving neighbor.

Jackie Koss: Jackie, you make me laugh and feel good. You are so smart, you can do anything, and you don't mind telling people what is on your mind. We became great friends while working at basketball camp at Tennessee. You drove all night to be with me the first full week that I was in the hospital. You stayed with me several times during my treatments. You were a godsend because of your background in oncology at Vanderbilt but most importantly because of your friendship.

Gina Markland: Gina, we met at Pat Summitt's Basketball camp at Tennessee in the late seventies. From Asheville, North Carolina, you're a great coach and now an administrator at Coastal Carolina University. You're a great gal who is so trustworthy. We both love the beach and enjoy spending quiet time together. Always ready to help, Ms. Dependable.

Kathy Streeter Morgan: "Streeter," we met each other at the American Red Cross National Aquatics School at Camp Rockmont in Black Mountain, North Carolina, in 1976. We have been great friends ever since then. You were the first point guard for Coach Kay Yow at Elon College. You're a wonderful friend who can do everything (and I mean everything), except play the piano! I think you recently decided to take piano lessons, just to master something else.

Sheila Oliver: You and I have only been friends for about four years. You interviewed me for a book, and that was all it took. You were helping me with my memoir and almost had it finished when I was diagnosed with AML. You're a retired librarian and did most of the research for this book. Thanks, Sheila, for all your hard work. This book would not have happened without you.

Ralph Rhyne: My brother, Ralph, one of the greatest guys in the world. A great person and a great brother. Ralph, you remind me of my parents, especially my mother. You have a heart of gold and love your big sisters, Phyllis and Sylvia. It is an honor to have a little brother like you. Your wife Karen is also a jewel of a person, smart, and an aggressive worker, always looking to help other people. The two of you take care of my mountain house.

Paula Ryan: My crazy, funny, smart, shag dancing, beach friend. When I'm around you, I laugh so much that my stomach hurts. I never know what you're going to say. You're a great shagger, the top realtor in North Myrtle Beach, and a strong-willed woman with a heart of gold.

Judy Stroud: A basketball guru and friend from way back, you are an awesome gal who loves the game and has been a great player, coach, and referee. We have been great friends for many years. When I got leukemia, you came running to my assistance. You did not care about the politics that could be involved, and we both kept it very professional. It meant the world to me.

- SOURCE MATERIAL -

Chapter 1

"I don't look at this moment as a defining..." from "Jordan inducted into Hall of Fame", *BBC*, September 12, 2009, and available at http://news.bbc.co.uk/sport2/hi/other_sports/basketball/8252243.stm

Chapter 2

"There are always new, grander challenges..." from *Go For The Goal: A Champion's Guide to Winning in Soccer and Life* by Mia Hamm, Harper Collins, 2013, page 6.

"A godly woman 'in the center of God's will...'" from *Prayer the Great Adventure* by David Jeremiah, Doubleday Religious Publishing Group, 2004, page 218.

Chapter 3

"In Sleep we lie all naked and alone..." from *A Stone, a Leaf, a Door: Poems* by Thomas Wolfe, Scribner, 1969.

Chapter 4

"When you die, that does not mean that you lose..." from "ESPN SportsCenter Anchor and Dedicated Family Man Stuart Scott has Passed Away", *ESPN*, January 4, 2015, and available at http://espnmediazone.com/us/press-releases/2015/01/espn-sportscenter-anchor-and-dedicated-family-man-stuart-scott-has-passed-away/

Chapter 5

"The metaphor for it metastasizes, too..." from *Impossible Bottle: Poems* by Claudia Emerson, LSU Press, 2015.

"Sylvia Hatchell is temporarily stepping away..." from "UNC coach Hatchell temporarily stepping aside due to health reasons", North Carolina Athletics, October 23, 2013, and available at http://www.ncaa.com/news/basketball-women/article/2013-10-14/unc-coach-hatchell-temporarily-stepping-aside-due-health

Chapter 6

"Most of the time we think we're sick..." from *Look Homeward, Angel* by Thomas Wolfe, Simon and Schuster, 2006, page 10.

"Problems are only opportunities with thorns..." available at http://www.wisdomquotes.com/quote/hugh-miller.html

"Worry does not empty tomorrow of its sorrow..." from *Clippings From My Notebook* by Corrie Ten Boom, Triangle, 1982.

"The only thing we can do is play on the one string..." available at https://www.goodreads.com/author/quotes/5139.Charles_R_Swindoll

"Don't limit yourself..." available at https://www.goodreads.com/author/quotes/24453.Mary_Kay_Ash

Chapter 7

"I encourage my players to treat games..." from *Hard Work: A Life On and Off the Court* by Roy Williams, Algonquin Books, 2011, page 213.

Chapter 8

"Fight! We Fight for Alma Mater..." available at http://library.unc.edu/music/uncsongs/

Chapter 9

"I think the real free person in society is one that's disciplined…" from *A Coach's Life: My Forty Years In College Basketball* by Dean Smith, Random House Publishing Group, 2000, and available at http://www.brainyquote.com/quotes/quotes/d/deansmith617933.html

"Only in the storm can you see the art…" from *Not All Bad Comes to Harm You* by Janice Mock, iUniverse, 2015.

Chapter 10

"Live. Fight like hell…" from "Here's Stuart Scott's Brilliant ESPYs Speech About Fighting Cancer", *Business Insider*, January 4, 2015, and available at http://www.businessinsider.com/stuart-scott-speech-2015-1

"Difficult times always create…" from *Real Moments* by Barbara De Angelis, Delacorte Press, 1995, page 145.

"Successful people are always looking…" available at http://www.goodreads.com/quotes/23000-successful-people-are-always-looking-for-opportunities-to-help-others

Chapter 11

"If you make every game a life and death proposition…" available at http://www.brainyquote.com/quotes/quotes/d/deansmith190901.html

"Whatever I am, whatever I will become…" from "Hollywood Faith Facts: Elvis Presley", *BeliefNet*, July 1, 2015, and available at http://www.beliefnet.com/Entertainment/Galleries/Hollywood-Faith-Facts-Elvis-Presley.aspx?p=4

Chapter 12

"We're not retreating, we're just advancing…" from *Ways of War: Amer-*

ican Military History from the Colonial Era to the Twenty-First Century by Matthew S. Muehlbauer and David J. Ulbrich, Routledge, 2013, page 430.

"This is how sad my life is..." available at http://www.brainyquote.com/quotes/quotes/l/lewisblack583592.html

Chapter 13

"You know when you're young..." quoted in *With A Day Like Yours, Couldn't You Use A Little Grace* by Megan Rohrer, lulu.com, 2014, page 187.

Chapter 14

"I firmly believe that in every situation..." available at http://www.beliefnet.com/Quotes/Entertainment/A/Andy-Griffith/I-Firmly-Believe-That-In-Every-Situation-No-Matte.aspx

"The most important day of your life..." quoted in *How to Succeed in the Game of Life: 34 Interviews with the World's Greatest Coaches,* Diversion Books, 2015.

Chapter 15

"I think if there's a great depression..." quoted in *A Global Green New Deal: Rethinking the Economic Recovery*, Cambridge University Press, 2010.

"Velcro (sticking and holding) and our positive..." from "Alternative Orthodoxy: Week 2, Turning Toward the Good" by Richard Rohr, February 18, 2016, and available at https://cac.org/turning-toward-the-good-2016-02-18/.

Chapter 16

"Our old ordinary means nothing here..." from *Impossible Bottle:Poems* by Claudia Emerson, LSU Press, 2015.

Chapter 17

"My attitude is that if you push me towards..." quoted in *Winning Words: Classic Quotes from the World of Sports*, Taylor Trade Publications, August 1, 2008.

"God's definition of success..." from *Quiet Strength: The Principles, Practices, and Priorities of a Winning Life*, Tyndall House Publishers, Inc., 2011.

Chapter 18

"Peace fell upon her spirit..." from *You Can't Go Home Again*, Simon and Schuster, 2011, page 271.

Afterword

"As soon as you try to describe a close friendship..." available at http://www.brainyquote.com/quotes/quotes/d/deansmith539342.html.